SPREADING
THE
FLAME

SPREADING THE FLAME

CHARISMATIC CHURCHES AND MISSIONS TODAY

Edward K. Pousson

FOREWORD BY C. PETER WAGNER

ZondervanPublishingHouse

Academic and Professional Books

Grand Rapids, Michigan

A Division of HarperCollins*Publishers*

Spreading the Flame
Copyright © 1992 by Edward K. Pousson

Requests for information should be addressed to:
Zondervan Publishing House
Academic and Professional Books
Grand Rapids, Michigan 49530

Library of Congress Cataloging-in-Publication Data

Pousson, Edward K.
    Spreading the Flame / Edward K. Pousson.
       p.   cm.
    Includes bibliographical references and index.
    ISBN 0-310-53331-7
    1. Pentecostalism. 2. Missions. I. Title
    BR1644.P68 1992   91-29004
    289.9–dc20
                                    CIP

Edited by John Vriend and Leonard G. Goss
Cover designed by Terry Dugan Design

Printed in the United States of America

92 93 94 95 96 / CH / 10 9 8 7 6 5 4 3 2 1

To
LAI KHENG
faithful companion in
marriage and ministry
and
JACHIN EDWARD & JUSTICE KEITH
my beloved sons

Contents

CHAPTER 1
A HINGE POINT IN HISTORY: CHARISMATIC
CHURCHES MEET THE MISSIONARY CHALLENGE | 21

Charismatics Come of Age
Realizing the Reason for Revival
Creating New Patterns of Ministry for a New World

CHAPTER 2
ORIGINS OF INDEPENDENT
CHARISMATIC CHURCHES | 33

Healing Revivalists Sow Seeds of Independence
Charismatics React Against Institutional Churches
Testimony Gives Way to Teaching
The Story of the Loyalists and the Separatists
New Patterns of Ministry Reach New People

List of Figures

Foreword

The closing decade of the twentieth century is shaping up to be, in the opinion of many observers, the decade of the greatest outpouring of the Holy Spirit around the world—at least in living memory. The harvest has never been riper. Year after year more people are becoming Christians, and more Christian churches are being multiplied than ever before. The book of Acts appears as a mere pilot project compared to what God is doing today.

An increasingly visible and influential component of all that God is doing is what we know as the independent charismatic movement. This movement, which David Barrett calls the Second Wave, is now the fastest-growing segment of Christianity in many sectors of the world, the United States included. While its beginnings can be traced back to the 1960s, the great growth spurt of the independent charismatic movement began in the early 1980s. Already, in a surprising number of world-class cities, the largest Christian church in the city is independent charismatic.

Independent charismatics are warm-hearted, Bible-believing Christians. Because of that they have a God-given passion for evangelizing the world. They sincerely want to be instruments of God for carrying the Gospel to the lost.

But while the desire has been there, the cross-cultural missionary ministries of independent charismatics have not yet reached their potential. This is due somewhat to the independent part of their designation. The rapidly increasing number of independent charismatic churches and denominations (which they prefer to call fellowships or networks) can accurately be described as "new wineskins." But while much progress has been made on developing internal structures for local churches and associations of churches, little energy has been expended on doing it for vehicles aimed at world evangelization.

Edward Pousson enters the scene at this point. He belongs to an independent charismatic local church, he is part of one of the networks of such churches, and he has served as a career cross-cultural missionary in Africa and Asia. In addition to these credentials he has also become a trained missiologist with a doctorate in the field. Few people I know could be as well qualified to write *Spreading the Flame*, the book you are about to read.

This book does what no other has done. It describes how the independent charismatic movement came into being, what makes it tick, and where it may be headed in the future. But that is just background for a thorough explanation of what missionary vision the leaders have, of what experimental structures have already emerged to implement foreign missions, and of questions that need to be answered in order to do it better. Ed Pousson is not afraid to identify weaknesses as well as strengths. This is not to say he is a critic. He is more like a coach. He wants the team to which he belongs to be all that God wants it to be.

This is a meaty book. But it serves up good-tasting meat. The more you read, the more you will want to read and the more excited you will become about the future for charismatic missions in particular and for the kingdom of God in general. Ed Pousson will help you put your finger on the pulse of God and feel his heartbeat for world missions as you have never felt it before. It will bless you and subsequently make you a blessing to many others.

> — C. Peter Wagner
> Fuller Seminary School of World Mission
> Pasadena, California

Acknowledgments

To my wife, Lai Kheng. She emboldens me to attempt things beyond my natural ability and helps me accomplish what I would never attempt on my own.

To my pastor, Rod Aguillard, and home church, Reserve Christian Fellowship, in Reserve, Louisiana. Their loving prayers and generous financial support remained steadfast through the years of study and research that stand behind this book.

To C. Peter Wagner; his wife and secretary, Doris; and other School of World Mission professors at Fuller Theological Seminary in Pasadena, California. This study was inspired by their life-changing insights and facilitated by their practical guidance.

To my friend and editor at Zondervan Publishing House, Len Goss, and to my other friends at Zondervan, Stan Gundry and Ed van der Maas. Their patient assistance and expert advice made this project possible.

Introduction

We see from church history that renewal movements have often produced significant missionary movements. The early Pentecostal movement is a case in point. But what sort of missionary movement has the charismatic renewal produced? This is an exciting, unfolding drama, the story of which is waiting to be told.

This book represents an opening chapter in the story of charismatic missions. It tells of the exciting growth and development of independent charismatic churches—an aspect of the charismatic renewal virtually overlooked by scholars until recently. Most of the literature deals with charismatic renewal *within* mainline churches.

This book also describes a variety of charismatic missionary models and developments that will inspire and challenge both charismatic and noncharismatic readers. It suggests some guidelines for further unleashing the powerful—but sometimes latent—charismatic missionary force into the world today.

The central concern of this study, then, is to describe, analyze, and evaluate the missionary activities of certain independent charismatic churches and ministries based in the United States. The term "independent charismatic" refers to a specific group. First, these are churches and ministries that have participated in the charismatic or neo-Pentecostal movement that began in the 1950s and flourished in the 1960s and beyond. Second, these are churches and ministries that, due to their charismatic experiences and innovative philosophies of ministry, either have left their denominations or have recently formed, free of denominational ties.

Many churches from various backgrounds fit this description. Since their emergence in the late 1960s, they have continued to multiply. Current scholarly estimates put them at 60,000 to 100,000 in number in the United States. Some whom I have identified as belonging to this group may not like the charismatic label. But what sets them apart for our concerns is the fact that they have embraced certain aspects of the charismatic renewal and are consequently not institutionally aligned with classical Pentecostalism or any other denominational tradition.

Even more significantly, we zero in on these new congregations because their nondenominational stance often leaves them with no formal ties to organized mission boards. Thousands of these churches simply lack the overarching mission structures needed to mobilize their numbers and resources in effective cross-cultural evangelism and church planting. In missiological terms, much of the independent charismatic movement is a churchly movement without a missionary arm. From this arises their need to create new missions structures if they are to participate significantly in world evangelization in obedience to the Lord's command to make disciples of all nations.

Therefore this study of charismatic missions seems timely. It ventures into a vast, uncharted field of recent American church and missions history, asking pertinent questions such as, Where did these independent charismatic churches come from? How can we categorize them in terms of major ecclesiastical streams? What is crucial in the history and culture of this movement for an understanding of its current missions situation? How do the basic tenets of charismatic theology help or hinder obedience to the biblical missionary imperative? How can we integrate charismatic theology with a biblical theology of missions?

Equally important are questions of structure and strategy: What are the major bottlenecks hindering missions mobilization among independent charismatic churches? What new models of missionary outreach have they forged in place of discarded denominational programs? What are the strengths and weaknesses of their approach?

The big question behind all these questions is this: How might charismatics more effectively unleash their massive missionary potential upon the three billion people of this world who have yet to hear, believe, and obey the Gospel?

Our quest for answers holds special significance for independent charismatic churches that are just beginning their missions involvement or are yet to begin. Missions interest is stirring among charismatics, and many are looking for successful charismatic models. But books on independent charismatic missions have been slow in coming, except for a few biographies. The whole story begs to be told. We need to spotlight the pioneers of charismatic missions so that others, charismatics and noncharismatics alike, might be informed and challenged to make their greatest possible contribution to the task of discipling all peoples to Christ.

Generalizing from a sampling of charismatic missionary patterns, I offer a representative picture of the missiological situation among independent charismatic churches in the United States. For example, while some groups have started their own extra-local missions sending agencies, others have developed what we will call the sending church model, in which the local church sees itself as the missions agency. This model is comparable to that of the Churches of Christ and the Plymouth Brethren, whose approach to missions will be examined for its relevance to the charismatic sending church.

Because of the vast diversity in the independent charismatic church phenomenon, some groups will not identify with my conclusions. But I believe the questions and issues themselves will prove relevant to many missions situations. I have presented the issues and findings in a form suitable for introducing charismatics to contemporary missiological principles so as to challenge them to greater and more effective harvesting of the masses yet to be added to the church.

Although this study is based on research, I write on a popular level, appealing to a variety of readers and especially to independent charismatics, the fastest-growing segment of the American church today, according to C. Peter Wagner, a leading authority on church growth. Charismatic ministers and laypeople are becoming more and more interested in missions. An increasing number of charismatic churches are hiring missions directors and sending out homegrown missionaries. This study is intended to inform and to challenge this burgeoning missions force to greater efficiency.

Both denominational charismatics and noncharismatic observers of the movement will also be interested in this study. It offers a challenge to churches and missions agencies in general. For example, the charismatics' Spirit-centered theology of missions, their emphasis on miracles, and their need-*oriented approach to evangelism will provide insights useful to all who labor to reach the unreached for Christ.

My personal interest in this subject stems from my past involvement in developing new missions structures for independent charismatic churches. The goal of this study is to help such churches further realize their massive missionary potential, plan more effective missions strategies, and mobilize their vast resources to make their greatest possible contribution to the unfinished task of world evangelization.

A Hinge Point in History: Charismatic Churches Meet the Missionary Challenge

---

Chapter 1

We are at a point in history when, more than ever before, the fulfillment of the Great Commission is within reach. In our hands rests the possibility of giving today's three billion non-Christians a valid opportunity to accept Jesus Christ as their Lord and Savior. This global opportunity beckons the involvement of the whole church, independent charismatics included.

Independent charismatics, we have seen, are those who have left their parent churches and formed or joined new, nondenominational churches which espouse charismatic patterns of ministry and worship. Due to their rapid growth and robust faith, these churches abound in available missionary personnel, finances, and zeal for missions. But, while charismatics in mainline churches usually serve under ready-made missions boards, many independent charismatics have no such links to organized missions bodies. On the local level they often lack the structures and strategies needed to unleash their missionary potential. There are growing indications, however, that charismatic churches are coming of age, coming to terms with missions as the reason for revival, and coming up with new and creative models for effective missionary outreach.

CHARISMATICS COME OF AGE

As mentioned before, the charismatic renewal has left tens of thousands of independent churches in its wake. There are about fourteen million nondenominational charismatic Christians in North America alone, according to missions researcher David Barrett.[1] Along with many others, I desire to see this rapidly growing movement release more of its vast resources for spiritual harvest among the nations.

The Cessation of the Manna.   As we move toward and into the twenty-first century, we need to grasp our critical place in missions history. We are at a moment in time when, more than ever before, the church has the money, people, technology, and tools needed to evangelize the world. The late 1980s were characterized by a growing sensitivity to the new challenges of our world, and Pentecostal-charismatic leaders were among those calling for a mature response to the signs of the time.

In July 1988, for example, Jack Hayford, pastor of the Church on the Way in Van Nuys, California, urged charismatic leaders at a Network of Christian Ministries conference in Anaheim, California, to begin trusting God for a new kind of miracle—warfare miracles. Many charismatics have been lulled to sleep with a loaves-and-fishes kind of faith. We are still feeding on "manna." But as Hayford urged, we are at a turning point in history where the manna is ceasing—meaning we are no longer on the crest of charismatic revival. It is now time to "put away childish things," such as an undue preoccupation with our own needs and wants. It is time to meet the "Captain of the Lord's host," who not only heals our diseases and meets our needs, but who also wants to enlist us in his army, to lead us in battle against Satan's strongholds.

Hayford's charge summons a hope for a new generation of Joshua-type leaders who will take the independent charismatic movement "across Jordan," so to speak, to reap great harvests from the world's twelve thousand unreached people groups still needing missionaries today.

Marks of Maturity.   Among many signs of maturity in charismatic churches, two are outstanding: a trend toward unity, and a growing evangelistic urgency. All across the nation, thousands of independent charismatic leaders and churches are linking together in networks or loose associations, such as Oral Roberts' Charismatic Bible Ministries and the Network of Christian Ministries, currently led by Paul E. Paino of Calvary Temple Worship Center in Fort Wayne, Indiana. Networking allows ministers to unite and cooperate without denominational ties.

But unity is not an end in itself. Along with other perceptive charismatic leaders, Charles Simpson sees this "God-inspired season of unity" as a platform for "worldwide proclamation of the gospel with spiritual power."[2] This focus on unity *for* missions is spreading among charismatic leaders and signifies that we are coming to terms with the real purpose of our twentieth-century Pentecost.

REALIZING THE REASON FOR REVIVAL

"When are we going to do it?" asked a newly converted rock musician. "Do what?" came the reply. "Go out and tell the people about Jesus and heal the sick as he did and cast out demons. . . ." Anglican charismatic leader Michael Harper tells this story to illustrate the link between renewal and evangelism.[3]

World missions seems to be woven into the fabric of spiritual renewal. The first Pentecost produced a mighty missionary movement that swept across the then-known world. The worldwide missionary outreach launched from Elim Bible Institute in New York can be traced back to the Finney revival of 1830.[4] And the Pentecostal revival in the first half of this century spawned an unparalleled, worldwide expansion of the Christian faith. The Spirit that renews the church is by nature a missionary Spirit.

Renewal starts with an inward focus that revitalizes the church. But to keep in step with the Spirit, renewed churches must sooner or later turn their attention to evangelism and missions. Many charismatic churches are now approaching this turning point. We have come to realize that the "end" of revival is the "ends" of the earth and that the mantle of spiritual power is tied to the mandate of world missions. Churches that frustrate this ultimate reason for revival are courting spiritual stagnation. In fact, according to Howard Foltz, founder of the Association of International Missions Services (AIMS), lack of mission is a known stifler of charismatic fellowships.[5]

Meeting the Missionary Challenge. Charismatics have been criticized from many quarters for their "lack of mission." David J. Hesselgrave, Professor of Mission at Trinity Evangelical Divinity School, reports this encounter with a Pentecostal leader:

> One highly placed and respected Pentecostal leader recently reminded me that the Charismatic movement as such has never given birth to a significant missionary thrust. Moreover, he insisted that the missionary emphasis of the 1987 General Congress on the Holy Spirit and World Evangelization. . . represents a Pentecostal influence in the planning committee, not a Charismatic one.[6]

I fully agree with this concern. But fairness demands the concession that some of this concern arises from the fact that recent charismatic missionary activities are largely undocumented. This is especially true in the case of independent charismatics, where a closer look shows that many of their churches and leaders are urgently taking hold of the missionary challenge.

For example, some networks of churches are founding their own missions agencies. In 1986 I helped organize Gulf States Missions Agency. This charismatic mission recruits, trains, and sends out missionaries from a large network of charismatic churches known as the Gulf States Fellowship, based near New Orleans, Louisiana. Some of the larger churches, such as Bethany World Prayer Center in Baton Rouge, Louisiana, have the resources to operate their own church-based missions programs. On the other hand, many missionaries launch out from parachurch missions structures, such as Ken Sumrall's Globe Missionary Evangelism based in Pensacola, Florida.[7]

Hundreds of creative charismatic missions structures are multiplying throughout the United States.[8] Most exciting of all, the charismatic-oriented Association of International Missions Services (AIMS) now links many of these new and varied forces for missions together in a network of strategic cooperation and shared information.

Such developments signify a mighty ground swell of missionary interest and activity in independent charismatic churches today.[9] How effective are these efforts? Despite what critics might call "untidy tactics," we can thank Pentecostal and charismatic missions for some eighty percent of all current conversions from paganism to Christianity, according to David Barrett.[10]

Supplying the Missing Link. The charismatic missionary drive is also evidenced by the global evangelization goals being set for A.D. 2000. In 1987 Southern Baptist missions researcher Jimmy Maroney challenged a group of charismatic leaders with these words:

> If the Great Commission is to be completed by A.D. 2000, you Charismatics must play a principal role. As I travel the world, I see Charismatics everywhere. You have a ready-made network of people with faith and vision . . . who operate in the supernatural. You are the missing link to completing all the A.D. 2000 plans.[11]

Today several Pentecostal and charismatic groups are advancing global missions drives oriented to the A.D. 2000 theme. In 1988, for example, a group known as Charismatics United for World Evangelization initiated plans and processes aimed at providing all persons on earth the opportunity to hear the Gospel by A.D. 2000.[12] The North American Renewal Service Committee (NARSC), led by Vinson Synan, has the second largest of some eighty active A.D. 2000 global evangelization plans.[13] In August 1990 NARSC spearheaded the North American Congress on the Holy Spirit and World Evangelization, which met in Indianapolis with the intent of launching the 1990s as a decade of evangelization. Renewal leaders felt that the congress, with its theme "Evangelize the World Now!" marked a turning point in Pentecostal and charismatic renewal.

The final night of the gathering witnessed eighty percent of the nearly twenty-three thousand participants standing and asking God to use them in world outreach.[14] Jimmy Maroney can now rejoice. The "missing link" is finding its place in God's global plan.

CREATING NEW PATTERNS OF MINISTRY FOR A NEW WORLD

When the Gospel as we package it loses its edge in a changing society, God sends revival to chisel away outdated patterns of ministry and evangelism. New patterns of ministry then break out, impacting new segments of society, and exposing worn-out Christians to the real power of the Gospel. The charismatic renewal illustrates this.

In the 1950s, for example, Demos Shakarian broke the stained-glass barrier and took the Gospel into the banquet halls. This banquet evangelism gave spiritually cool businessmen a chance to window shop the charismatic experience without "going to church." Then Shakarian's Full Gospel Business Men's Fellowship exported the charismatic experience to the ends of the earth.

In 1969, when Oral Roberts saw that he was losing the masses to television, he shook the sawdust from his shoes, folded his tent, and fine-tuned his message for the TV audience with prime-time religious variety shows. In the next few months his mailing list grew by 300,000 new names.[15] He began reaching all sorts of people who had lost touch with the reality of the Gospel. These examples, as well as Chuck Smith's outreach to Jesus people and David Wilkerson's ministry to drug addicts, show how God uses the dynamics of renewal movements to bring the church's ministry methods up-to-date with an ever-changing society.

The combination of a changed world and a renewed church also impacts missionary methods. Some old patterns remain useful, but new patterns emerge. For example, when Bob Weiner saw that hundreds of tomorrow's world leaders now were studying on America's campuses, he organized

Maranatha Campus Ministries (MCM). MCM's parent organization, Maranatha Christian Churches, was restructured in early 1990, but the campus outreach continues.[16] This charismatic organization not only witnesses to foreign students, but wins them to Christ, trains them, and sends them back to their own countries as indigenous church-planting missionaries.

Does it work? In 1986 twenty Indonesian students who had been won and trained in America went home as a ready-made indigenous church and transplanted themselves into Indonesian soil. Within a few months they grew to 342 members, according to Mark Kyle, formerly of Maranatha.[17] This is representative of the new and diverse missionary patterns emerging from charismatic circles today.

While these and other bright beginnings in charismatic missions are laudable, we cannot ignore apparent shortcomings. In the area of stewardship, for example, while Pentecostals and charismatics in 1988 gave $34 billion to Christian causes, or $1.97 per member per week, only 15 cents per member per week went to global foreign missions, according to David Barrett.[18] This stewardship failure shows how modern American materialism has made its mark on a movement that, at the turn of the century, began among the poor and lower classes of society. This point is revisited in chapter 8, where we look at our movement in light of certain anthropological insights.

The earlier chapters of this book are historical in character, focusing on the origins and aspects of independent charismatic churches and the trend toward networking of churches under prominent apostolic leaders. Chapters 6 and 7 identify, analyze, and evaluate a selection of charismatic missionary models in the light of contemporary church growth principles. Much of what we call "missions" does not really create new churches or add new disciples to existing churches. Vast numbers of independent charismatic churches have yet to forge links with mission agencies or to develop their own missions outreach. Chapter 9 brings aspects of the biblical theology of mission to bear upon major tenets of charismatic theology. The missionary mandate running through the whole Bible needs to move closer to the center of charismatic teaching and preaching.

A Moment in Time. The opportunity for world harvest has never been greater. Even though some countries are closed to professional missionaries, it has never been easier for Christians to visit and live in other countries. For the first time in history, potential missionary sending churches now exist in nearly every nation on earth. These and other world changes are reordering the missionary landscape. The melt-down of the Iron Curtain, for example, has already called forth new missions strategies on the part of certain charismatic churches. Combining mass evangelism with church planting techniques, Larry Stockstill, pastor of Bethany World Prayer Center in Baton Rouge, Louisiana, recently planted two indigenous churches in Russia.

Paul Pierson, missiologist and dean of Fuller Theological Seminary's School of World Mission, observes that we are at a major hinge point in history.[19] The economical, political, and spiritual center of gravity is shifting to a broader, multinational context. Japan, South Korea, and Singapore, for example, are emerging as major economic and political leaders on the world scene.

On the spiritual scene, the non-Western missionary movement will soon be the world's largest and most powerful missionary force, given its rapid growth rate. In 1988 there were 85,000 Western missionaries and 36,000 missionaries from the Third World. But by the year 2000, if current trends continue, there will be 162,000 non-Western missionaries as compared to 136,000 from the West, according to Larry Pate, leading authority on Third World missions.[20]

These and other global changes are mentioned in chapter 10. Such developments will drastically impact missions strategies. More new and varied patterns will emerge. Those who discern the times and forge new methods of ministry and missions will survive the transition and reap great harvests. There are encouraging signs that independent charismatics will be among those on the front lines of the new era of missions.

To echo the words of a wise old Jew who knew his times, "who knows whether you have not come to the kingdom for such a time as this?" (Est. 4:14, RSV).

NOTES

[1]David B. Barrett, "Statistics, Global," in Stanley M. Burgess and Gary B. McGee, eds., *Dictionary of Pentecostal and Charismatic Movements* (Grand Rapids,: Zondervan, 1988), pp. 817, 827. David Shibley estimates that there are 80,000 independent charismatic churches in America. See Shibley's book, *A Force in the Earth* (Altamonte Springs, Fla.: Creation House), p. 29. Jim Ammerman, founder of Chaplaincy Full Gospel Churches, Dallas, Texas, estimates that there are 100,000 independent charismatic churches in the United States.

[2]Bruce Longstreth, ed., "The Year of Equipping the Saints," interview with Charles Simpson, et al., *New Wine*, Vol. 18, No. 1, Jan. 1986, p. 14.

[3]Michael Harper, "Renewal for Missions: An Anglican Perspective," *International Review of Missions*, Vol. 75, No. 298, Apr. 1986, pp. 129–30.

[4]Anthony Cardinale, "From Elim to the World," *Charisma & Christian Life*, Vol. 13, No. 3, Oct. 1987, p. 86.

[5]Howard Foltz, "Bottlenecks Hindering Mission Mobilization," *Ministries*, Vol. 4, No. 3, Summer 1986, p. 41. Foltz is the founder of the Association of International Missions Services, a major independent charismatic missions organization. His observation about charismatic fellowships and lack of mission is credited to Robert Wild's book, *The Post Charismatic Experience* (Hauppauge, N.Y.: Living Flame Press, 1984), p. 128.

[6]David J. Hesselgrave, *Today's Choices for Tomorrow's Mission* (Grand Rapids: Zondervan, 1988), p. 128.

[7]I use the term "parachurch" lightly, and by way of capitulation to standard terminology. However, my conviction is that these structures are just as much within and part of the "church" (overall body of Christ) as are local churches. Furthermore, Globe Missionary Evangelism is fully oriented toward local churches and would probably not consider itself parachurch. Globe is further described in chapter 7.

[8]Barrett, "Statistics, Global," p. 830.

[9]Historian Peter D. Hocken (Ph.D., University of Birmingham) makes a most striking observation in his article "Charismatic Movement," in Burgess and McGee, eds., *Dictionary*. On p. 157 he writes, "The strongest consistent missionary thrust among charismatics has come from restorationist 'non-denominational' circles and from para-

church groups with a strong charismatic membership, such as Operation Mobilization and the Pentecostal-originated YWAM. . . ."

[10]Barrett's claim is cited in Vinson Synan's article "Global Consultation on Evangelization: A.D. 2000 the Target," *A.D. 2000 Together*, Vol. 3, No. 1, Spring 1989, p. 7. Other researchers have documented findings that lend credence to Barrett's claim. See Larry Pate, *From Every People* (Monrovia, Calif.: MARC, 1989), p. 129; and C. Peter Wagner, *Spiritual Power and Church Growth* (Altamonte Springs, Fla.: Strang Communications, 1986), p. 12; and Wagner, *How to Have a Healing Ministry Without Making Your Church Sick* (Ventura, Calif.: Regal Books, 1988), pp. 68–89.

[11]Maroney quoted by Howard Foltz in "Moving Toward a Charismatic Theology of Missions," *Probing Pentecostalism* (Society for Pentecostal Studies, 17th Annual Meeting, Nov. 12–14, 1987, CBN University, Virginia Beach, Va.), p. 73.

[12]Barrett, "Statistics, Global," p. 830.

[13]Vinson Synan, "Global Consultation," p. 7. For more data on the number of active A.D. 2000 plans, see Ralph Rath, "700 Evangelization Plans," *A.D. 2000 Together*, Vol. 3, No. 1, Spring 1989, pp. 8–10.

[14]Timothy K. Jones, "Charismatics Shift Gears at Indianapolis Assembly," *Christianity Today*, Vol. 34, No. 13, Sept. 24, 1990, pp. 48–49. See also Steven Lawson, "Ready to Evangelize the World," *Charisma & Christian Life*, Vol. 16, No. 3, Oct. 1990, p. 24.

[15]David E. Harrell, Jr., *All Things are Possible* (Bloomington, Ind.: Indiana University Press, 1975), pp. 148–49, 155.

[16]See Stephen Strang, ed., "Maranatha Revamps Church Structure," *Charisma & Christian Life*, Vol. 15, No. 8, Mar. 1990, p. 21.

[17]Mark Allen Kyle, *World Ambassadors: An Exciting Adventure in World Missions* (Gainesville, Fla.: Mark Allen Kyle, 1987), p. 52.

[18]Barrett, "Statistics, Global," pp. 811, 830; 814–15.

[19]Interview, February 28, 1989.

[20]Larry Pate, *From Every People* (Monrovia, Calif.: MARC, 1989), pp. 45, 51.

Origins of Independent Charismatic Churches

---|---

Chapter 2

But now tongues have moved uptown," wrote David Wilkerson in 1973.[1] "This pentecostal thing . . . jumped the wall," said one old-time revivalist.[2] And "some 2,000 Episcopalians are said to be speaking in tongues in Southern California," wrote Frank Farrell in 1963.[3]

About thirty years ago, Episcopal clergyman Dennis Bennett went public about his "Nine o'clock in the Morning" charismatic experience. Since then barrels of ink have documented the dynamics of the charismatic renewal that began in the 1950s and mushroomed in the 1960s. And while most of the literature deals with the penetration of Pentecost *within* the historic churches, few authors have grappled at length with the independent charismatic church movement.[4]

Figure 1 helps clarify what we mean by independent charismatics and where they fit in the overall Pentecostal-charismatic movement. The "m" stands for millions, and these numbers are based on estimates by researcher David Barrett.[5] The fine line represents the so-called *first wave* of the Spirit, the Pentecostal movement, which began at the turn of the century. This includes classical and other Pentecostal denominations.

The double line is the *second wave*, the charismatic movement, which began in the 1950s and flourished in the 1960s and beyond. The 140.5 million charismatics in 1990 include both mainline charismatics (eighty-two percent) and independent or nondenominational charismatics (fourteen percent). The remaining four percent are made up of Messianic Jewish charismatics and what Barrett calls radio and television charismatics.

The medium-sized line on the graph shows the growth of the *third wave*, a current movement mainly in Protestant denominations where many are adapting certain Pentecostal-

GLOBAL EXPANSION OF THREE WAVES
OF RENEWAL OVER TWO DECADES

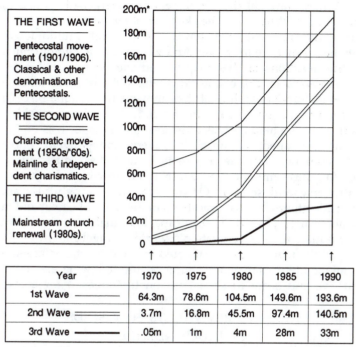

	THE FIRST WAVE
Pentecostal movement (1901/1906). Classical & other denominational Pentecostals.	
THE SECOND WAVE	
Charismatic movement (1950s/'60s). Mainline & independent charismatics.	
THE THIRD WAVE	
Mainstream church renewal (1980s).	

Year	1970	1975	1980	1985	1990
1st Wave ————	64.3m	78.6m	104.5m	149.6m	193.6m
2nd Wave =====	3.7m	16.8m	45.5m	97.4m	140.5m
3rd Wave ————	.05m	1m	4m	28m	33m

* m = million

Figure 1

charismatic experiences within their own theology and worship.

We have stressed the phenomenal growth of the independent charismatic movement, the fastest-growing segment of American Christianity. From 1970 to 1988, independent charismatics averaged fourteen percent of the total charismatic renewal (the second wave). They number twenty million worldwide and some fourteen million in North America alone, according to Barrett.[6] But the story of how and why these nondenominational churches emerged is, to many, an untold story. And if you happen to belong to one of these churches, this is your story.[7]

Where have all these independent charismatic churches come from? What are the key spiritual dynamics of the charismatic renewal that birthed this great multitude of churches? What are they like? And where are they going? Such are the questions of this chapter and the next.

Answers to these questions will help insiders achieve further self-understanding of their movement's unique place in the charismatic renewal and in church history. These considerations will also help curious outsiders gain perspectives on the origins and aspects of those phenomenal independent charismatic churches. But the real issue behind these questions is this: Are these churches an abnormal outgrowth of charismatic controversy and schism? Or do they have a rightful place alongside other Christian traditions in the body of Christ and in salvation history? And are they capable of making a significant contribution to this generation's world evangelization?

Of the many causes that could be cited for the emergence of independent charismatic churches, the following are representative and seem to shed light on their reason for being.

HEALING REVIVALISTS SOW SEEDS
OF INDEPENDENCE

Many of today's independent charismatic ministries have their immediate antecedents in the healing revival of the 1950s. Oral Roberts, T. L. Osborn, Jack Coe, and scores of other prominent healing revivalists were affiliated with various Pentecostal denominations. But they kept their evangelistic associations relatively free from the control of their churches. Their Pentecostal supporters eventually began to frown upon their independence and ministry methods. Finally, the inevitable clash came.

Many of the healing evangelists, including Oral Roberts, broke from the Pentecostal bodies and broadened their ministry and support base to include non-Pentecostal churches. The Full

Gospel Business Men's Fellowship helped them rise to prominence on this new turf. Through ballroom evangelism and television broadcasting, they were able to influence segments of the church and society that were generally cool toward classical Pentecostals. And their ministries bridged certain elements of Pentecostalism into mainline churches. This was a key impetus behind the charismatic renewal.[8]

This also sowed seeds of independence which have now come to fruition in the form of thousands of independent charismatic churches. In fact, as Vinson Synan puts it, "Many of these churches originated under the influence of [Oral] Roberts' pioneering ministry while some others are led by graduates of Oral Roberts University."[9] Similarly, hundreds of independent churches have flowered under the ministry of Kenneth E. Hagin, Sr., whose roots also go back to the healing revival of the 1950s.

CHARISMATICS REACT AGAINST INSTITUTIONAL CHURCHES

> Those who must wait for organizational sanction upon every new sign of God's presence will find themselves hesitating in the pews of skepticism while courageous men and women of faith advance and do exploits in His name.[10]

T. L. Osborn penned these words in his magazine, *Faith Digest*, in June 1956. This attitude was typical of the healing evangelists of the day. In fact, this strong current of independence spans the entire Pentecostal-charismatic movement. Every major stream of the renewal seems to produce its own breed of independent churches.

For example, Derek Prince, Bob Mumford, and the other Fort Lauderdale gentlemen who led the discipleship and shepherding movement of the 1970s made independence the norm. In the words of historian Charles E. Jones, they "declared the church radically independent of ecclesiastical structures."[11] As the shepherding model of ministry caught on, it produced hundreds of independent charismatic churches in

North America and Great Britain, according to Jones. Anti-institutional sentiments took hold in other charismatic quarters as well, producing various types of independent churches.

TESTIMONY GIVES WAY TO TEACHING

In the 1960s the charismatic renewal was essentially a decentralized, reformist movement with a focus on renewing the historic churches. Charismatic prayer meetings concentrated on worship, charismatic gifts, healing, and testimonies. Moving into the 1970s, however, the renewal spawned a generation of charismatics thirsty for more of the Spirit and for more intimate relationships with each other. More significantly, these people wanted deeper teachings on the Spirit-filled life than what could be found in their historic churches.[12]

Certain leaders of the renewal, namely Derek Prince and his Fort Lauderdale co-workers, sensed this need for deeper teaching and moved in to fill the vacuum. They founded the Holy Spirit Teaching Mission, which later became Christian Growth Ministries.[13] Other important centers of teaching and influence came to national prominence, such as the Episcopal Church of the Redeemer in Houston, Texas, and Ralph Wilkerson's Melodyland Christian Center in Anaheim, California.[14]

This shift toward teaching raised the central question of authority. Should renewed Christians submit to local pastors and priests, or to trans-local shepherds and teachers? Where should they send their tithes? These and other tensions threatened the unity of the charismatic renewal. As Anglican renewal leader Michael Harper puts it, "People began to assert that the new wine of the Holy Spirit could not be contained in the old bottles of the historic churches."[15] Scores of new independent charismatic churches and teaching centers emerged in the wake of the controversy. More and more established churches were losing their members to these new wineskins.

THE STORY OF THE LOYALISTS
AND THE SEPARATISTS

In the initial stage of the renewal the "in thing" was to stay in one's church and help renew it.[16] For example, in the mid-1950s, James Brown, a Presbyterian pastor in Philadelphia, received the charismatic experience and spoke in tongues. Initially he thought about leaving his church. But first he asked the famous Pentecostal leader David du Plessis what he should do. Du Plessis told him, "Stay in your church and renew it." Brown stayed in his church and carried on a successful renewal ministry for more than two decades, according to Vinson Synan.[17] Many other well-known charismatic leaders have stayed in their churches to help renew them. Examples include Dennis Bennett (Episcopal), Harald Bredesen (Lutheran), Larry Christenson (Lutheran), Tommy Tyson (United Methodist), and Gary Clark (American Baptist).

For many other charismatic leaders it was not so easy. In 1958 John Osteen, a Southern Baptist pastor in Houston, Texas, received the Pentecostal experience, tongues and all. This was through contact with a local Assembly of God pastor. For almost one year, Osteen tried to stay in his church and renew it. But growing opposition eventually forced him out. With about one hundred loyal followers, he founded Lakewood Baptist Church in 1961. Lakewood Church, as it is called today, is now an independent charismatic church with about twenty thousand members. This church has launched an effective missions outreach to more than one hundred nations of the world.[18]

Hundreds of other early Southern Baptist charismatic leaders who spoke openly of their Pentecostal experience shared Osteen's rejection experience. In many cases, the schism produced new churches. Prominent examples of such churches include those pastored by Lester Sumrall, Jamie Buckingham, and Larry Lea (although Lea's role in his church became more "apostolic" than pastoral in 1990).

This same dynamic was paralleled in other denominations, especially those opposed to the renewal. Of course, not all of the nonconformist churches have grown as fast as Osteen's. But positive growth has occurred, and many new independent churches have sprung into existence throughout the United States, some as separatists, and many others planted independently from the beginning. Thus, among the factors contributing to the rise of independent charismatic churches, schism seems to be a leading cause.

Strangely enough, the word "schism" occurs in church-growth authority C. Peter Wagner's list of positive charismatic growth factors.[19] Often there is a spiritual dynamic at work here. The late J. Edwin Orr, an authority on renewal movements, likened a church split to an alley-cat fight. Two cats meet in the alley. They are alone when the fur begins to fly. But when it is all over, the alley is full of new cats.

Does God then endorse church splits? Probably not anymore than he does cat fights. But he often works through church splits in such a way that, when the dust settles, each side grows faster than the two of them did when they were together, according to Wagner. So the scourge of schism is counterbalanced by the virtue of diversity. Each group can now tailor its appeal to differing segments of the community. This means a larger number of unchurched people will be exposed to the Gospel.

NEW PATTERNS OF MINISTRY
REACH NEW PEOPLE

Oral Roberts and hundreds of other ministers were on the cutting edge of the healing revival of the 1950s. But few of them were able to stay on the crest of the wave as it surged forward into the charismatic renewal. As we have shown, Roberts is one of the survivors. Why? Because he knew when it was time to fold the tent. He discerned the times, forged new patterns of ministry suitable to a new social tapestry and sensitive to the new move of the Spirit. Historian David E. Harrell, Jr., sums it up poignantly:

God was moving in new ways. Some clung to the old methods and supporters; others accepted the new challenge. Some of the evangelists could adapt their healing message to the Hilton ballroom; others needed sawdust under their feet.[20]

This illustrates an important spiritual principle that underlies this entire book: Renewal movements usually give birth to new forms of ministry that are free of outdated tradition, compatible with new social and cultural conditions, and consonant with the current move of God's Spirit. The phenomenal rise of independent churches is preeminently rooted in this spiritual dynamic.

This probably underlies most other factors behind the rise of these churches. Most of the "Jesus people" of the 1970s, for example, could not be folded into traditional churches, even Pentecostal ones. Chuck Smith tried it and it did not work. So God raised up new kinds of churches, such as Smith's Calvary Chapel and Bob Weiner's Maranatha churches, to harvest and disciple vast numbers of these young people. You will also find droves of them, along with other "baby boomers," wearing blue jeans and T-shirts, worshiping in John Wimber's Vineyard churches and other similar fellowships that cater to the youth culture.[21]

Traditional churches still appeal to large segments of society, young and old. But God needs as many different kinds of churches as there are different kinds of peoples in the world. There is plenty of room for denominations as well as "nondenominations." And the independent charismatic churches that are reaping vast portions of the Lord's harvest today are playing a crucial role in salvation history. They have a rightful place alongside other established church traditions in the church at large.

These churches have weaknesses and strengths, as the next chapter shows. But given their massive numbers, resources, and spiritual vitality, they stand to make a great contribution toward the global completion of the Great Commission in our generation.

NOTES

[1]David Wilkerson, *David Wilkerson Speaks Out* (Minneapolis: Bethany Fellowship, 1973), pp. 15f. Quoted in Vinson Synan, *Aspects of Pentecostal-Charismatic Origins* (Plainfield, N.J.: Logos International, 1975), p. 222.

[2]See David Edwin Harrell, Jr., *All Things Are Possible* (Bloomington, Ind.: Indiana University Press, 1975), p. 145.

[3]Frank Farrell, "Outburst of Tongues: The New Penetration," *Christianity Today*, Vol. 7, No. 24, Sept. 1963, p. 1163.

[4]One exceptional article on these churches is Stephen Strang's "Nondenominational Pentecostal and Charismatic Churches," in Stanley M. Burgess and Gary B. McGee, eds., *Dictionary of Pentecostal and Charismatic Movements* (Grand Rapids: Zondervan, 1988), pp. 638ff. Strang describes essential characteristics of these churches and gives many illustrative examples. In this chapter I am primarily concerned with the dynamics of the renewal that birthed these churches.

[5]Barrett, "Statistics, Global," in Burgess and McGee, eds., *Dictionary*, pp. 812–13. Notes on terminology used in figure 1: At first the charismatic movement of the 1960s was called the neo-Pentecostal movement. Later, when Catholic neo-Pentecostals wanted to distinguish themselves from earlier Pentecostals, they began referring to the movement as the charismatic renewal. The term "classical Pentecostals" was coined to refer to the earlier Pentecostals. Leading scholars today see Pentecostalism as one outpouring of the Spirit having three major distinguishable streams or waves. Classical Pentecostalism is the first wave of the movement. It takes in churches like the Assemblies of God, the Church of the Four-Square Gospel, the Church of God (Cleveland, Tennessee), and many others. The second wave is the move of the Spirit within the Catholic Church and in established Protestant denominations. This is normally called the charismatic renewal. I follow this delineation in this book. Independent charismatic churches belong to the second wave. The third wave is the present move of the Spirit primarily in established Protestant churches where many are embracing the fullness of the Spirit in their own way and emphasizing spiritual gifts. Third-wavers generally do not identify with the labels or cultural trappings of Pentecostal-charismatics, and they have their own distinctive theologies about the Holy Spirit and his gifts. For more on the third wave, see C. Peter Wagner, *The Third Wave of the Holy Spirit* (Ann Arbor, Mich.: Vine Books/Servant Publications, 1988); and Wagner, *How To Have a Healing Ministry Without Making Your Church Sick* (Ventura, Calif.: Regal Books, 1988).

[6]On these figures, see C. Peter Wagner, "Church Growth" (pp. 181f, 192), and Barrett, "Statistics, Global" (pp. 812–15, 820). Both of these articles are in Burgess and McGee, eds., *Dictionary*.

[7]This is not a history of the charismatic renewal. I am primarily interested in the independent charismatic church phenomenon as the immediate backdrop of the missionary thrust emerging from these churches. Readers unfamiliar with the history of the charismatic movement should consult standard works such as the following: Michael Harper, *Three Sisters* (Wheaton, Ill.: Tyndale, 1979); Harrell, *All Things Are Possible*; Richard Quebedeaux, *The New Charismatics II* (San Francisco, Calif.: Harper and Row Publishers, 1983); Vinson Synan, *In the Latter Days* (Ann Arbor, Mich.: Servant Books, 1984); and Vinson Synan, *The Twentieth-Century Pentecostal Explosion* (Altamonte Springs, Fla.: Creation House, 1987).

[8]These developments are thoroughly documented and analyzed by Harrell in *All Things Are Possible*, pp. 5, 53–83, 107–16, 135–93. See also Walter J. Hollenweger, *The Pentecostals: The Charismatic Movement in the Churches* (Minneapolis: Augsburg, 1972), pp. 6–7, 35–38.

[9]Vinson Synan, "Oral Roberts: Serving Fellow Ministers," *Charisma*, Vol. 11, No. 9, Apr. 1986, p. 82.

[10]T. L. Osborn, "Concerning Our Association with The Voice of Healing," *Faith Digest*, June 1956, p. 17. Quoted by Harrell in *All Things Are Possible*, p. 65.

[11]Charles E. Jones, "Integrity Communications," in Burgess and McGee, eds. *Dictionary*, p. 460.

[12]See Michael Harper, *Three Sisters*, p. 92.

[13]See Michael Harper, *Christianity in Today's World* (Grand Rapids: Eerdmans, 1985), p. 103; Harrell, *All Things Are Possible*, pp. 184f; and Quebedeaux, *The New Charismatics II*, pp. 135–42 (especially p. 139).

[14]While Melodyland Christian Center was founded in the late 1960s, it was during the early-to-mid-1970s that it rose to national prominence. See Burgess and McGee, eds., *Dictionary*, p. 600; and Harrell, *All Things Are Possible*, p. 184.

[15]Michael Harper, *Christianity*, p. 103.

[16]Quebedeaux, *The New Charismatics II*, pp. 11, 82–84, 154.

[17]Vinson Synan, *The Twentieth Century Pentecostal Explosion*, (Altamonte Springs, Fla.: Creation House, 1987), p. 164.

[18]See Stephen Strang, "Osteen, John Hillery," in Burgess and McGee, eds., *Dictionary*, p. 656. See also, Synan, *The Twentieth Century Pentecostal Explosion*, pp. 25–29.

[19]C. Peter Wagner, "Church Growth," in Burgess and McGee, eds., *Dictionary*, p. 194.

[20]Harrell, *All Things Are Possible*, pp. 148–49.

[21]See Synan, *In The Latter Days*, pp. 121–23.

Independent Charismatic Churches: Blessing or Babel?

———+———

Chapter 3

Independent charismatic churches? They are like a bunch of live wires on the loose. Sometimes you think somebody rang a fire alarm during the worship service. Only you do not hear the alarm, and you do not see the fire. You just see the effects. I once took a rustic, red-haired mechanic to one of these churches—my home church, in fact. I had been witnessing to Ken and God was dealing with him. It turned out to be one of those "fire alarm" services. So I decided to step out for a drink of water. And when I came back in, wouldn't you know it! The whole church was doing a "Jericho march" around the sanctuary. "Oh no," I thought, "why did this have to happen tonight?" I just knew Ken would be turned off.

End of service: "Well, Ken, uh. . . what did you think?" I asked. "I liked it," he said, "it's GREAT!" He was beaming. I dared not ask, but I think he had even joined the march. That was 1983. Today, Ken is still a faithful member of Reserve Christian Fellowship, that fiery Full Gospel church in Reserve, Louisiana. Babel? Or blessing?

Independent charismatic churches, like it or not, are here to stay. As I have repeatedly emphasized, they are the fastest-growing segment of American Christianity, with some fourteen million believers attending eighty thousand or more newly-formed churches in the United States.[1]

What, then, are we to make of these churches? Are they playing a positive and significant role in the body of Christ as a whole? And what contribution are they making toward world evangelization? In short, is the independent charismatic church movement a blessing from heaven or just a babel of "charisma-nia"?

Thinking people can see that independent charismatic churches have their shortcomings. But it also needs to be seen that many of the major weaknesses spring from "withdrawal symptoms" and "fast-growing pains" that is, problems that result from rapid, spontaneous growth *apart* from the usual structural and theological helps provided by denominations.[2] In many ways, our independence has worked to our advantage, but there are some side effects.

WITHDRAWAL SYMPTOMS

Some of the problems are petty, but others are potentially fatal. I am concerned only with the latter. The issues I raise here are not criticisms, but challenges. Some of them are addressed in greater detail in later chapters. As charismatics honestly face these issues, they stand a better chance of becoming and remaining an effective force for worldwide renewal and harvest.

1. Baptizing the American Dream. The first challenge has to do with our relationship to American cultural values. The early Pentecostal movement was a counterculture movement, a religion of the masses, denouncing worldliness and appealing to blue-collar workers and to the poor. Ray Hughes, former head of the Church of God (Cleveland, Tennessee) says: '

> Most of us classic Pentecostals came from the blue-collar, working-class group. And the thing that made Pentecostalism grow was that they took the Gospel to the poor. We must never forget our roots, regardless of how the Gospel has lifted us materially.[3]

The second wave of the Spirit, the charismatic renewal, was more culture affirming, spreading to the American middle class, and gradually accommodating its values.[4] But the road to respectability was costly. What Pentecostals once labeled as vices, many now sanction as virtues.[5] An authority in religious studies, Grant Wacker writes,

> Describing the latter aspect of contemporary Pentecostalism as a "veritable spiritual Amway movement," historian

> David Edwin Harrell notes that it offers not healing for the
> sick, but security for the well; not consolation to the poor,
> but confirmation to the successful.[6]

A certain amount of cultural accommodation is essential for a greater harvest. The apostle Paul said, "I have become all things to all men so that by all possible means I might save some" (1 Cor. 9:22b). To be "good news" the gospel must appeal to the felt needs of particular peoples. But when this is overdone, it dulls our prophetic edge and alters our understanding of the gospel. Missiologists call this syncretism. And that is what seems to be happening in some charismatic circles as well as in other parts of the American church, especially in the area of material wealth.

No one more than I believes and embraces the biblical promises of health and abundance. But once we allow a materialistic rights-consciousness to replace cross-bearing servanthood, we are in danger of baptizing the American dream. The "gospel" we preach with our lives then will fail to penetrate and challenge the culture at a deep level. Furthermore, we will lose touch with the poor masses, where the needs are great and the harvest is ripe. Lest I sound one-sided here, a later chapter will further develop this theme, showing how charismatics have also challenged their culture in significant ways.

2. *Structural Shortcomings.* "Sustained creativity requires enough structure to follow through on ideas," writes charismatic leader and author Jamie Buckingham.[7] Spiritual ministry, no matter how gifted, needs some structure in order to fulfill its potential and perpetuate itself. For example, the oldest and largest classical Pentecostal bodies in the world today, the Assemblies of God, the Church of God (Cleveland, Tennessee), and the Church of God in Christ, are those that early on struck a balance between spontaneity and structure, spiritual leading and strategic planning.[8] In fact, it was largely a drive to bring order to an independent Pentecostal missionary explosion that led to the birth of the Assemblies of God denomination in 1914.

But the charismatic exodus from denominations leaves many new churches with too little structure. Without links to organized missions agencies, many churches are falling far below their missionary potential. The lack of local church missions planning and the lack of a cooperative missions structure are among the "major bottlenecks hindering missions mobilization" on the part of charismatic churches, according to Howard Foltz, founding president of the Association of International Missions Services (AIMS).[9] These and other matters of missionary structure will be addressed in more detail in later chapters.

3. *Abuses That Kill.* Lack of structure affects more than our missionary outreach. Numerous problems have shown that independent charismatics lack effective means for holding ministers in mutual accountability. Too many preachers have indulged in extreme individualism, affluence, hype, high-pressure fund-raising tactics, and a kind of triumphalism that smacks of pride and self-exaltation. This charismatic vice list is deliberately selective and strangely ominous. For these are precisely among the major abuses that killed the postwar healing revival, according to the trained eye of historian David E. Harrell, Jr.[10]

4. *Theological Shortcomings.* In a movement as diverse and fast growing as the charismatic movement, mature theological reflection often lags behind a proliferation of new "revelations" and trendy teachings. Russell Spittler, Assemblies of God minister and professor of New Testament at Fuller Theological Seminary, notes,

> The charismatic movement as a whole is doctrinally unpredictable, at times marked and marred by a Corinthian elitism. . . . [But] Moral convictions often lag behind religious conversion.[11]

We can only hope that in due time charismatics will tidy up their theology where they need to. In the meantime, however, trends and fads tend to undermine effective missions involvement. "The fulfillment of God's mission on earth certainly is not 'trendy,'" writes Howard Foltz.[12] To counter the neutralizing effect of trendiness, charismatics need a nation-wide missions education and awareness drive. Solid convictions based on a sound, biblical missions theology should supplement our zeal and enthusiasm if we want to advance to the forefront of the worldwide missionary movement that is now on the horizon.

5. *Stalling in the Upper Room.* "We've been in the upper room with our spiritual gifts. But we are supposed to go to the streets with our tongues and healings and prophecies." Vinson Synan gave this charge at the New Orleans 1986 Leaders' Congress, which was a forerunner to the New Orleans 1987 Congress on the Holy Spirit and World Evangelization.[13] It reflects the birth pangs of a charismatic shift from "being blessed" to "becoming a blessing" to all nations, in accordance with the mandate of God's covenant with Abraham in Genesis 12:1–3. But many of our churches are still in the "bless me" stage. A shortsighted focus on the home front blurs our vision to carry the light to the nations. Signs and wonders often become ends in themselves instead of a means of witness to the ends of the earth as Acts 1:8 commands.[14]

These and other problems inevitably have gone along with the explosive growth that broke denominational seams and created legions of new churches. But that is not the whole picture. The fruits of the charismatic renewal combined with the ecclesiastical freedom of the independent churches give them certain assets that seem to vindicate their right to exist alongside other major forces in Christendom.

CHARISMATIC STRONG POINTS

Some of the positive characteristics of the independent charismatic church movement that make it a major force for ongoing church renewal and worldwide missionary advance are as follows:

1. *Combating Postcharisma.* A major dilemma is confronting renewal leaders within mainline churches today. These leaders often devote most of their energies to renewing their own churches.[15] Despite their noble efforts, however, a revolving-door syndrome undermines mainline church renewal. After about two or three years of involvement in charismatic prayer groups, most Catholics and mainline Protestants begin to lose interest and become what David Barrett calls "postcharismatics." Based on Barrett's estimates, more than half of the 140 million charismatics around the world today are actually postcharismatics.[16] This does not necessarily mean that they are less committed to Christ. But they are no longer consistently involved in the charismatic movement. Given this dilemma, the visible fruits of the renewal could eventually slip through the fingers of the historic churches.[17]

This postcharismatic phenomenon points up the significance of the role being played by independent charismatic churches today. This is where the charismatic renewal is growing the fastest. Like new wineskins for new wine, these churches serve as a necessary, nondenominational expression of the renewal, preserving the fruits of the movement, and acting as a catalyst for ongoing renewal of traditional churches. Some independent charismatic ministries, such as Pat Robertson's Christian Broadcasting Network, have already proved to be effective bridges for renewal in historic churches. Their nondenominational stance is a key to their success.[18]

2. *Becoming One in Diversity.* Some observers deplore the fragmentation and rampant sectarianism that prevail in some charismatic quarters.[19] Beneath this babel of diversity, however, there is an underlying unity centered on the Lordship of Jesus and the activity of the Holy Spirit. I have visited charismatic churches in several states and in several countries. There is a prevailing spirit of unity at work in these churches. Despite the diversity and the disconnectedness between many churches, there is a kind of sameness, a oneness that is seen as a direct work of the Holy Spirit.

In the late 1980s "shepherds" of the discipleship era,

namely Charles Simpson and Bob Mumford, began linking arms with prosperity teachers in what has been called a unity movement.[20] Bob Mumford's public apology in November 1989 for his part in the discipleship/shepherding movement opens the way for a new era of unity and for the final healing of the great charismatic rift of the 1970s, when the lines were drawn between shepherding leaders and other prominent charismatic figures.[21]

These factors allow for the current nationwide and international networking of tens of thousands of charismatic churches—the subject of the next chapter. And while charismatic leaders do not want to create new denominations, there is a move toward structural cooperation in ministry and world missions. For example, the Association of International Missions Service (AIMS), a charismatic organization, unites groups together around a single purpose, cooperation in world evangelization. One can only hope that this trend toward unity and networking will counter some of the more serious problems related to independence.

3. *Doing Theology That Works.* Outsiders criticize charismatic theology and sometimes even ridicule it, but they have to admit that it works.[22] Independent charismatic churches bring theology into the service of ministry rather than binding their ministry to some form of traditional orthodoxy. They honor the Scripture as sacred, but they boldly address their theology to the real, felt needs and questions of the people to whom they minister.

Church-growth authority Carl George, for example, makes this observation:

> The "market" has become open to supernatural manifestation. The American population is increasingly open to the supernatural and the Charismatics have a theology for coping with the supernatural in the present world, while older denominations see miracles as occurring in Bible times.[23]

This "working theology" is one of the reasons for the rapid growth of independent charismatic churches. Missiologists call this "contextual theology." Contextualizing theology usually involves some risk of syncretism or heresy. However, it is essential to the communication of the faith across cultures and from one generation to the next. Contextual theology applies the essentials of the Gospel in a way that is relevant to the thought patterns, questions, concerns, and felt needs of a given society or people group.[24]

True contextual theology, however, must be linked both to the Bible and to historical theology. If a choice had to be made, however, many charismatics would rather brave the threat of heresy, where churches are growing and miracles are flowing, than to sit on the ice of orthodoxy with the "frozen chosen." This may be offensive to some noncharismatic evangelicals, but it is merely an observation of what seems to be a prevalent attitude.

4. *Unleashing the Laity.*   Three months after my 1975 conversion from the rock music scene, I joined an independent charismatic church in Reserve, Louisiana, a small town on the bank of the Mississippi River near New Orleans. On my first visit, I was wearing a pullover shirt, bell-bottom jeans with frayed cuffs, and a worn-out pair of mountain climbing boots. I had long hair and smelled of strawberry incense.

During that first service, despite my attire and aroma, the pastor put me on the platform and let me "minister" in music with my beat-up Gibson guitar. Within a few weeks I was teaching Sunday school and doing street evangelism in the community. After three years the church leaders laid hands on me, gave me a prophecy, and sent me off to the mission field, first to Haiti, then to Ghana, and finally to Malaysia. Four years later I came back and was put on staff as an associate pastor in the church. All of this, *before* I went to seminary!

My story illustrates a typical pattern for leadership training in independent charismatic churches. They do not prize informality or ignorance, but they do recruit and train people on the basis of divine calling and spiritual gifts, rather than formal seminary training. Churches with multiple ministry staff often recruit and train their staff from among their own people. And most charismatic churches rely heavily upon trained lay leaders who carry much of the load on a voluntary basis.[25]

For example, Victory Christian Center, an 8,000-member independent charismatic church in Tulsa, Oklahoma, has only thirty people on the pastoral staff. The rest of the work is done by volunteers who put in eight hours a day, two or three days a week.[26] Similarly, Fred Price's 16,000-member charismatic church in Los Angeles, California, has a "helps ministry" of 1,500 to 2,000 volunteers and only 200 to 250 salaried employees, including elementary and junior high school staff and teachers.[27]

This combination of homegrown staff with volunteer personnel insures a smooth team ministry by people who share a common vision and philosophy of ministry. Not only is this a key to healthy growth, but it also gives people a sense of worth, purpose, and fulfillment as they discover and use their spiritual gifts for the upbuilding of the church to the glory of God. This eager volunteerism also holds promise for a vast pool of potential missionary recruits.

5. *Supplying Laborers for World Harvest.* A basic assumption of this book is that great outpourings of the Spirit usually generate great forward movements of the faith. The Holy Spirit is a missionary Spirit. This dynamic prompts one of the major questions of this book: What kind of missionary movement has the charismatic renewal produced? Further research and documentation is needed, but already we know that charismatics in all segments of the church represent a viable, active force for missions.

Research has shown that charismatics are among the most successful missionaries and church planters. Because of this, missions boards of some denominations, including the Anglican Communion, actively recruit charismatics from their ranks, according to Vinson Synan.[28] Documenting renewal in the Mennonite Church, Synan writes, "Today practically all the

Mennonite missionaries of the world have received the Baptism in the Holy Spirit and these mission fields are blazing areas of evangelism."[29]

Gary Clark, leader of the American Baptist Charismatic Fellowship, was told by a denominational leader that about one third of the American Baptist Church's missionaries have had a charismatic experience and that many of these people are among the denomination's most effective missionaries.[30]

But what about independent charismatic missions? Consider this striking quote from historian Peter D. Hocken:

> The strongest consistent missionary thrust among charismatics has come from restorationist "nondenominational" circles and from parachurch groups with a strong charismatic membership, such as Operation Mobilization and the Pentecostal-originated YWAM [Youth With a Mission]. . . .[31]

Although YWAM does not label itself "independent charismatic," it absorbs by far the lion's share of the independent charismatic missionary force worldwide. An estimated fifteen percent of their 6,000 full-time workers and 25,000 annual short-termers are independent charismatics. Evidence is mounting that independent charismatic churches and missionaries are already among those on the forefront of world missions.

WHICH WAY NOW FOR INDEPENDENT CHARISMATIC CHURCHES?

The current move of the Spirit among independent charismatic churches seems to be toward networking and world evangelization. As the next chapter shows, various streams are flowing together in loose, overlapping associations such as the National Leadership Conference, led by Jim Jackson, and the Fellowship of Covenant Ministers and Conferences, formed in 1987 by Charles Simpson.[32] Leaders of these and many other networks are constantly on guard against the dangers of institutionalization.

Charismatic churches' organizational flexibility, lay-liberation, and multiple tracks to ministry and ordination make it easy for their members to rise from pew to pulpit. These churches are surging with an abundance of spiritual energy that can easily be channeled into evangelism and world missions. Their bold faith, vision, and ability to deal effectively with demonization make them especially suited to the missionary challenge in non-Western settings. Without a doubt, the independent charismatic church movement represents a major force for ongoing renewal in the church at large, and for evangelizing the world "by the power of signs and miracles, through the power of the Spirit" (Rom. 15:19).

NOTES

[1]David Barrett, "Statistics, Global," in Stanley M. Burgess and Gary B. McGee, eds., *Dictionary of Pentecostal and Charismatic Movements*, (Grand Rapids: Zondervan, 1988), pp. 814f, 827. See also David Shibley, *A Force in the Earth, The Charismatic Renewal and World Evangelization*, (Altamonte Springs, Fla.: Creation House, 1989), p. 29.

[2]See Richard Lovelace, "Evangelical Spirituality: A Church Historian's Perspective," *Journal of the Evangelical Theological Society*, Vol. 31, No. 1, Mar. 1988, p. 33. Lovelace writes, "The charismatic renewal continues to express the mystical spirituality of the Puritan and awakening eras, but often without the rational and theological checks against error and credulity maintained by evangelicals. As a consequence, charismatics have some of the problems of the radical spiritualists in the anabaptist and Puritan left wing." On this point, see also J. I. Packer, "Piety on Fire," *Christianity Today*, Vol. 33, No. 8, May 12, 1989, p. 21.

[3]Ray Hughes quoted in Grant Wacker, "America's Pentecostals: Who They Are," *Christianity Today*, Vol. 31, No. 15, Oct. 16, 1987, p. 21.

[4]For a thorough analysis of the "upward mobility" of American Pentecostalism, see Walter J. Hollenweger, "After Twenty Years' Research on Pentecostalism," *International Review of Mission*, Vol. 75, No. 297, Jan. 1986, p. 6; Richard Quebedeaux, *The New Charismatics II* (San Francisco: Harper & Row, 1983), pp. 17, 31–38, 108–9, 162–77; Vinson Synan, *Aspects of Pentecostal-Charismatic Origins* (Plainfield, N.J.:

Logos International, 1975), pp. 195–98; 222–25; and Wacker, "America's Pentecostals," pp. 20–21.

⁵Wacker, "America's Pentecostals." On page 21 he writes, "Pentecostalism has paid a steep price for moving uptown. Its uncritical identification with the values of middle America represents a major loss of prophetic vision." Commenting on the affluence of some modern Pentecostal televangelists, Wacker writes, "What it suggests, rather, is that Pentecostals tend to label as vices the things they cannot afford—until they can."

⁶Ibid.

⁷Jamie Buckingham, "Buckingham Report: Running a Tight Ship," *Ministries Today*, Vol. 5, No. 2, Mar./Apr. 1987, pp. 21f.

⁸See Richard Quebedeaux, *The New Charismatics II* (San Francisco: Harper & Row, 1983), p. 45; and Vinson Synan, *The Twentieth Century Pentecostal Explosion* (Altamonte Springs, Fla.: Creation House, 1987), pp. 15, 65, 75.

⁹Howard Foltz, "Bottlenecks Hindering Mission Mobilization," *Ministries*, Vol. 4, No. 3, Summer 1986, p. 42.

¹⁰David Edwin Harrell, Jr., *All Things Are Possible: The Healing and Charismatic Revivals in Modern America* (Bloomington, Ind.: Indiana University Press, 1975), pp. 138–44.

¹¹Kenneth S. Kantzer quoting Spittler in "Charismatics: Who Are We and What Do We Believe?" *Charisma*, Apr. 1980, p. 48. Kantzer is a former editor of *Christianity Today*. This article includes a quote from Thomas Zimmerman, former general superintendent of the Assemblies of God: "Assuming the commitment of those people to be genuine, it is my opinion that they will become orthodox evangelicals."

¹²Howard Foltz, "Moving Toward a Charismatic Theology of Missions," *Probing Pentecostalism* (Society for Pentecostal Studies, 17th Annual Meeting, Nov. 12–14, 1987, CBN University, Virginia Beach, Va.), p. 78.

¹³See Julia Duin, "Signs and Wonders in New Orleans," *Christianity Today*, Vol. 30, No. 27, Nov. 21, 1986, p. 27.

¹⁴See John Amstutz, "Dear Charisma," *Charisma*, Nov. 1985, p. 7; and Brian Bird (citing Ralph Winter), "Reach Every Nation: We Can Do It!" *Ministries*, Summer 1986, p. 30. Cf. David Shibley, "Why Pastors Don't Like Some Missionaries," *Ministries Today*, Vol. 6, No. 4, July/Aug. 1988. On p. 56, Shibley writes, "We must admit first of all that much of the American charismatic church is still in the 'bless me' stage, not realizing the 'why' behind their blessings." See also Shibley, *A Force in the Earth*, which shows that charismatics are now taking their global responsibility much more seriously.

¹⁵See Nick Cavnar, "Trend Toward Mature Unity," *Charisma*, Aug. 1985, p. 60. Cavnar writes, "With Charismatic leaders busy

working to strengthen their own ranks, its doubtful they will have much extra attention for efforts beyond their own churches."

[16]Barrett, "Statistics, Global," pp. 811–13, 826. For more on postcharismatics, see also, C. Peter Wagner, "Church Growth," in Burgess and McGee, eds., *Dictionary*, p. 183.

[17]See Peter D. Hocken, "Charismatic Movement," Burgess and McGee, eds. *Dictionary*, p. 144. According to Hocken, the charismatic renewal's fastest growth is in the independent charismatic church movement. Hocken says that the slowest growth of the overall Pentecostal-charismatic movement, however, "is in some sectors of [the charismatic renewal] within the historic churches. One implication is that the challenge of [the charismatic renewal] has not been addressed within the historic American churches as much as either denominational [renewal] leaders or church officials would like to think."

[18]Richard Lovelace, "Trend Toward Acceptance of Charismatics," *Charisma*, Aug. 1985, p. 100. See also p. 102, where Lovelace says, "Sociologist Jeremy Rifkin has suggested, in fact, that a new reformation in the historic churches could be led by Charismatics and evangelicals working together in balance. The former would supply a radical openness to the Spirit and Christian experience, while the latter would contribute reliance on the objective elements of faith: Scripture, tradition, reason, and practical method." Even though Lovelace and Rifkin may be speaking of charismatics in general, this statement supports the point made that independent charismatics play a key role in preserving the fruits of the charismatic renewal and sparking further renewal in denominational churches.

[19]See Packer, "Piety on Fire," p. 21.

[20]See Jean Coleman, "Network of Christian Ministries Meets in Denver," *Ministries*, Fall 1985, p. 98.

[21]See cover story and two related articles in *Ministries Today*, Vol. 8, No. 1, Jan./Feb. 1990, pp. 46–60. The controversy over the shepherding movement came to a head in the mid-1970s as one of the most violent controversies in charismatic history. Major figures in the renewal who opposed the shepherding movement were Kathryn Kuhlman, Demos Shakarian (Full Gospel Business Men's Fellowship International), Pat Robertson, and Jamie Buckingham. See "Shepherding Movement," in Burgess and McGee, eds. *Dictionary*, p. 783.

[22]See Michael Harper's discussion on the dynamic nature of charismatic theology in *Three Sisters* (Wheaton, Ill.: Tyndale, 1979), pp. 51–52.

[23]E. S. Caldwell quoting Carl George in "Trend Toward Mega Churches," *Charisma*, Aug. 1985, p. 35.

[24]See Paul A. Pomerville, *Pentecostalism and Missions, Distortion or Correction?* (Pasadena, Calif.: Fuller Theological Seminary, 1982), p. 7,

where he points out the importance of contextualizing theology and the grave consequences of failing to do so. On contextual theology, see also Dean S. Gilliland, *Pauline Theology and Mission Practice* (Grand Rapids: Baker, 1983), pp. 19–45; and Gilliland, ed., *The Word Among Us: Contextualizing Theology for Mission Today* (Irving, Tex.: Word, 1989).

[25]Cf. Caldwell, "Trend Toward Mega Churches," p. 38; and C. Peter Wagner, "What's Behind Charismatic Growth," *Ministries Today*, Vol. 6, No. 4, July/Aug. 1988, p. 51.

[26]Interview with Dolly Davis, missions secretary at Victory Christian Center, June 22, 1989.

[27]Telephone interviews with Gail Thompson of Crenshaw Christian Center's ministry of helps department, January 18, 1990, and January 30, 1990.

[28]Vinson Synan, "Pentecostalism: Varieties and Contributions," *Pneuma*, Fall 1986, p. 44. For other striking examples of the effectiveness of denominational charismatic missionaries, see Synan, *The Twentieth Century Pentecostal Explosion*, pp. 33, 34, 129.

[29]Synan, *The Twentieth Century*, p. 129.

[30]Ibid., p. 33. Also based on a 1986 interview with Clark.

[31]Hocken, "Charismatic Movement," p. 157.

[32]Ibid., p. 141f.

From Denominations to Networking: A Charismatic Megatrend

Chapter 4

Are you in the move of God?" It was a haunting question for Bob Mumford. "Yes. . . . of course," he answered the young woman. Yet he was not so sure, even though he was the Bible teacher at the camp meeting where she asked the question. Mumford tells the story in a 1986 issue of *New Wine*, where he lists several criteria for discerning "the move of God."[1]

One does not have to be an expert on the move of God today to know that in charismatic circles it has something to do with networking and unity among churches from various streams and backgrounds. But a charismatic who does not understand this, it is certainly possible that he may miss the move of God.

WHAT IS NETWORKING?

"Networking" became the buzz word of the eighties. In his book *Megatrends* (1984), John Naisbitt shows how a new model of management based on networking is replacing the centuries-old hierarchical, pyramidal leadership structure. The networking model works through informal, horizontal links between members of an organization who share ideas, information, and resources, in pursuit of common goals. This high-touch, people-oriented approach has proved successful in a number of large businesses, such as Honeywell, Intel Corporation, and Tandem Computer Company.[2]

Naisbitt identifies swirling changes of the 1960s and 1970s that helped foster the decentralized management trend. Rigid business hierarchies began halting under information overload. People rejected the cold impersonality of the technological age. America's economic empires and social institutions began switching over to a modern Japanese management style, in which small, decentralized working groups send decisions upward, instead of kowtowing to the traditional top-down decision-making process. In short, "The failure of hierarchies to solve society's problems forced people to talk to one another and that was the beginning of networks," writes Naisbitt.[3]

Through networking dynamics, "baby boomers" introduced movements such as the anti-war movement, the environmental movement, and the women's movement. Now ascending top-level management positions, baby boomers will probably never reconcile with yesterday's hierarchical leadership style.[4]

An Appropriate Sociology of Church Government. The social megatrend toward networking is also impacting the church. And nowhere is it seen more clearly than in the independent charismatic church movement. Since the 1970s, for example, charismatic groups have broken away from hierarchical denominations, forming thousands of new, independent churches.

In the middle to late 1970s, clusters of these churches began to form on the basis of personal relationships and networking between ministers. Examples of early networks include the International Convention of Faith Ministries in Tulsa, Oklahoma (with some one thousand ministers), other faith-oriented networks, and various groupings associated with the shepherding/discipleship movement. By the end of the 1980s, new networks were multiplying faster than researchers could document them. David Barrett speaks of as many as three thousand independent charismatic "denominations" by 1988.[5] As explained below, however, networks are not denominations in the strict sense of the word.

"Baby boomer" charismatics seem to have found in networking an appropriate sociology of church government for their generation. According to author and researcher Lyle E. Schaller, churches with little or no denominational affiliation are especially effective in attracting young adults born in the late 1950s and early 1960s.[6] John Naisbitt and Patricia Aburdene make a similar observation in their 1990 book, *Megatrends 2000*:

One reason large mainline churches have lost so many since the mid-1960s is that small, independent churches can adapt their services to the needs of churchgoers, can remain closer to the "consumer."[7]

Concerning the trend toward large churches, church growth authority Carl George says,

You will find very few large churches where the pastor is strongly tied to the programs of the denomination. They are men who are willing to do things differently. They are idea men; they are not imitators.[8]

Networking Versus Denominations. In some ways, charismatic networks function like denominations, even though they steadfastly avoid this label. How then are they different? I have looked at several major networks that are made up primarily of independent charismatic churches and ministries. What follows are some of the features that seem to distinguish them from denominations.

1. Loose, Overlapping Associations. Networks are loose associations of leaders and ministers of independent charismatic churches who relate to each other for the purpose of fellowship, mutual encouragement, and sharing of information, insights, and ideas. There are hundreds of networks all across the United States. Major examples include:

The International Fellowship of Faith Ministries (2,000 churches)

International Convention of Faith Churches & Ministries (495 churches; headquarters in Tulsa)

Faith Christian Fellowship International (1,000 ordained ministers)

National Leadership Conference (represents other networks)

Network of Christian Ministries (represents other networks)

Fellowship of Christian Assemblies (101 churches)

Fellowship of Covenant Ministers & Churches (250 churches)

Association of Vineyard Churches (290 churches)

Charismatic Bible Ministries (1,500 ministers)

Rhema Ministerial Association (525 churches)

Christ for the Nations (600 churches)

World Fellowship of Ministers (formed in 1991 by Charles E. Green of Word of Faith Church in New Orleans)[9]

There is considerable overlap between many networks, especially the larger ones. The National Leadership Conference, for instance, not only represents other networks but is itself a member of the Network of Christian Ministries. Sometimes prominent charismatic leaders hold executive positions in two or more networks. For example, at one time Jack Hayford, Kenneth Copeland, and Billy Joe Daugherty simultaneously served on the executive boards of both the Network of Christian Ministries, chaired by Paul Paino of Fort Wayne, Indiana, and Charismatic Bible Ministries, led by Oral Roberts.[10]

Usually only the ministers of a given network relate on a personal level, but their churches are linked together in kindred spirit. Networks do take in denominational churches, but independent charismatic ministers benefit most by joining. The primary focus is on unity and fellowship, but practical benefits include annual conferences, hotel and car rental discounts, monthly newsletters, tape clubs, ministry referral and placement services, membership transferrals, and the credibility of belonging to a larger group that stretches across several states. Some groups offer insurance and retirement plans for ministers. While some networks do license and ordain, ministers are usually credentialed on the local church level.

2. *Apostolic Leadership.* Networks are frequently led by groups of high-profile charismatic leaders whose ministries are recognized as having an apostolic dimension. Voluntary submission to their leadership is based on a combination of factors.

First, their authority is perceived as spiritual or derived from God, rather than legal or denominational. Second, they lead on the basis of "charisma," both in the biblical sense of the term (based on spiritual gifts) and in the sociological sense of the word. And third, their influence is bolstered by the visible fruits of their ministry. Network leaders are often pastors of large, dynamic churches and some have helped establish other churches.

Members of networks submit themselves to one another in varying degrees of mutual accountability. Some networks are more directive than others, but in most cases, local church autonomy is highly respected. For example, Oral Roberts writes concerning Charismatic Bible Ministries, "We have no intent to license or to ordain ministers, to govern individual bodies of believers in any way, or to censure. We recognize the sovereignty of each group."[11] This hands-off polity is one of the key factors behind the rapid growth of the independent charismatic church movement.

3. Nonbureaucratic, Nondenominational. "Charismatic Bible Ministries is not a denomination and does not plan to become one," writes Oral Roberts.[12] Some observers say that networks are, in effect, denominations, but insiders in virtually all major networks resist the label. As was mentioned earlier, many charismatics have come out of denominations. They know the difference between denominations and what is now called networking. There are no legal or formal ties between their members. The bonds are spiritual and relational, based on a common vision, common theological convictions, and similar philosophies of ministry.[13]

4. Groups Within Groups. Some of these groupings are actually networks of networks. For example, the National Leadership Conference, led by Jim Jackson of Montreat, North Carolina, links together several ministers who already serve various networks of independent charismatic churches.[14] The Network of Christian Ministries, for another, sees itself as an overarching structure, bringing together leaders and representatives from many different associations of charismatic churches.

Several major types or streams of charismatic networks can be distinguished from one another based on particular doctrinal and ministerial emphases. While there is much cross-pollination, most of the networks mentioned here can probably identify with one or more of the following types:

> Faith-confession and word churches (such as Kenneth E. Hagin's Rhema Ministerial Association)
>
> Covenant (discipleship/shepherding) churches (such as Charles Simpson's Fellowship of Covenant Ministers and Churches)
>
> Kingdom Now churches (such as Earl Paulk's Network of Kingdom Churches)
>
> Restorationist-charismatic churches (such as Larry Tom-czak's People of Destiny International)
>
> Some youth-oriented groups (such as John Wimber's Association of Vineyard Churches and Bob Weiner's Maranatha Christian Churches)

This list is by no means exhaustive, and John Wimber's Vineyard churches, with their emphasis on signs and wonders, may well belong in a category by themselves. But these are, nevertheless, representative of the kinds of groupings that seem to stand out amidst the sea of diversity that constitutes the independent charismatic church movement.

5. A Purpose Bigger Than Unity Itself. The networks described in Naisbitt's *Megatrends* work because they are made up of idea-driven people working together toward common goals. Some charismatic networks focus mainly on unity, fellowship, shared insights, and the practical and/or legal benefits of networking. But other networks are actively engaged in task-oriented cooperation toward specific ministry and mission goals.

For example, the Association of International Missions Services (AIMS), led by Howard Foltz, links churches and mission agencies together in a cooperative effort toward world evangelization. In 1988, B. J. Willhite formed the National Prayer Embassy in Washington, D.C., for the purpose of networking and mobilizing intercessory prayer groups all across the nation.[15] The Chaplaincy Full Gospel Churches, led by Jim Ammerman, is a network which has helped bring about the United States Pentagon's recognition of independent charismatic churches so that "Full Gospel" chaplains can now serve in the military. Chaplaincy Full Gospel represents about 1.5 million independent charismatics.[16]

These and other networks are actively moving beyond unity toward cooperation in specific ministry tasks. This is networking at its best. Biblical unity is not an end in itself. Jesus' priestly prayer for unity had world missions in mind: "May they be brought to complete unity to let the world know that you sent me and have loved them even as you have loved me" (John 17:23). To make a significant impact on world evangelization, networks need to combine and release their resources toward concrete ministry and mission objectives, such as those mentioned above.

WHY NETWORKING?

Many independent charismatic churches do not want to join networks, either because of strong convictions about local church autonomy, or perhaps because they have been wary of discipleship teaching.[17] As shown below, however, there are both spiritual and practical reasons why networking is a viable option for independent churches.

1. Networking, a Work of the Spirit. The ultimate reason for networking is that it seems to be the Lord's doing. Formerly divergent streams are now flowing together like rivers. Leading ministers from "discipleship" churches, "faith and word" churches, "kingdom now" churches, and others are linking together in overlapping associations. Kenneth Copeland calls this a "unity movement" and likens it to God calling the animals into Noah's ark just at the right time in history.[18] Many other charismatic leaders strongly feel that networking is a work of God among charismatic churches today.[19]

2. Biblical and Historical Precedents for Networking. God groups his people together in families. Israel's twelve tribes were large families, each having their own leaders and particular responsibilities. New Testament churches related to each other in a loose networking fashion, as Acts 15 shows. The apostle Paul planted autonomous churches, but he linked them together through his letters, apostolic messengers, and personal visits. And in large cities, such as Jerusalem, Antioch, and Rome, household-based groups made up different congregations of the broader urban church which occasionally met for corporate worship.[20]

Founders of early Pentecostal denominations saw the need to bring thousands of independent churches together into "loose associations." Individualism was getting old. Strange winds of doctrine were blowing everywhere. As Pentecostal researcher Walter J. Hollenweger documents, "all kinds of chaotic conditions" manifested themselves, "every man being a law unto himself."[21] Most of all, independent missionaries were launching out all over the world without proper support and legal recognition. These factors provided the motivation for the founding of the Assemblies of God as a "fraternal fellowship" for linking churches together and for supporting missionaries.[22] The recurrence of some of these conditions in certain charismatic quarters today confirms the need for networking and organizing for missions.

Early Pentecostal organizers did not intend the drift toward institutionalization which now threatens the vitality of some of those movements.[23] But, as noted in the last chapter, those groups that responded to the need for more structure and order are among the largest and fastest growing Pentecostal bodies in the world today. Other movements that resisted any kind of structure have largely dissipated.

Organization is not necessarily unspiritual. A certain amount of organization is essential for preserving and perpetuating the fruits of any movement. Many networks of charismatic churches today seem to be striking the right balance between the spontaneity of the Spirit and the need for structure.

3. *Practical Reasons for Networking.* Networking provides a check and balance against doctrinal extremes by bringing together representatives of various teaching emphases. As Kenneth Copeland puts it, " 'We know in part' (1 Cor. 13:9). But we have to get our parts together."[24]

Many small charismatic churches lack credibility in their communities because of their lack of identity with a larger group. Some ministers feel a sense of isolation—being the new charismatic kid on the block. Networking is one answer to these and other problems, such as the lack of ministerial accountability and the need for exposure to the larger Pentecostal-charismatic movement—not to mention the need for interaction with the larger evangelical movement.

The Internal Revenue Service's scrutiny of nonprofit religious organizations is another practical reason for networking. Some groups have formed with this need in mind. They provide legal coverage for smaller groups and churches seeking tax exempt status.[25]

4. *Networking Speeds Up World Evangelization.* Howard Foltz, president of the Association of International Mission Services, lists networking as one of seven keys for growing a missions church. He writes:

> Network with other churches and avail yourself of the services of reputable and experienced missions agencies. We need to avoid unnecessary duplication and also learn from both the positive and negative experiences of others.[26]

One of the strongest arguments for networking comes from the institutional base of the church growth movement—Fuller Theological Seminary's School of World Mission in Pasadena, California. While they deplore sectarianism and exclusivism, the late Donald A. McGavran and his successor, C.

Peter Wagner, have contended that multiplying new churchly associations will help speed up world evangelization.[27] God uses these new movements to help spark renewal in older churches and to win people to Christ who otherwise would not be reached by existing denominations because of the "stained-glass barrier"—social and cultural barriers unconsciously erected by the church itself as it loses touch with unchurched segments of society.

KEEP NETWORKS WORKING

As networks grow, structural innovations will become necessary if the independent charismatic church movement is to perpetuate itself and make an impact on world evangelization. However, the movement must guard against the negative forces of institutionalism that would threaten spiritual vitality and growth. Here are a few suggestions toward this end.

1. Stand Against Sectarianism. In 1988, the Network of Christian Ministries began calling forth and recognizing "apostolic fathers"—high-profile leaders who represent various streams and networks of independent charismatic churches, and who now sit together as one board of governors. These board members, about seventy in number, meet together annually as a "Congress of Elders" to address issues confronting the church and society.

As smaller networks multiply, this broad umbrella type of networking will provide a crucial safeguard against sectarianism. Because here is a structure where leaders of faith churches, covenant churches (discipleship), kingdom now churches, and others, including some classical Pentecostal groups, can meet and hear each other in an attitude of mutual respect and understanding.

2. Develop Accountability. The Network of Christian Ministries (NCM) has also implemented what they call the "tribal concept" in networking. As a network of networks, NCM does not seek to provide spiritual or legal coverage for its members. Instead, it refers members to smaller, established churchly associations or ministerial fellowships within the network. That way ministers relate in close-knit groups in which legal coverage is provided and where members hold each other accountable, exercising discipline as needed.[28] This is one example of how networking helps develop accountability on the part of independent charismatic churches and ministers.

3. *Keep Bureaucracy at Bay.* Networking values and dynamics can prevail, despite the degree of organization and structure introduced. Network leaders should empower individuals and groups to reach their own goals, rather than using them to advance a program merely for its own sake. Lines of communication can and should remain informal and horizontal. Ministers should maintain mutual accountability but preserve local church autonomy. Also, they should keep requirements for ministers on a spiritual track, rather than imposing rigid, formal educational demands. They should keep open several possible routes to ordination and ministry placement, rather than impose narrow, formalized requirements that have been known to halt church multiplication.[29]

C. Peter Wagner believes that when a network led by a single apostle grows beyond seventy-five or one hundred churches, it should consider forming two separate networks instead of one large one. The larger the network, the more complex the structure. With growing complexity comes the trend toward bureaucracy and hierarchy, a trend that tends to stifle further growth. This hypothesis is based in part on a study by Bill M. Sullivan of the Church of the Nazarene. Sullivan found that larger districts within the Nazarene Church experienced slower growth, while the smaller districts grew faster.[30]

4. *Form Smaller, Task-Oriented Groups Within Groups.* In order for unity among networking churches to become and remain functional, that is, have a purpose beyond unity itself, it is best to form smaller, task-oriented groups within the larger networks. For example, a given network may stretch across

several states and represent several hundred churches whose leaders meet together annually. Within such networks it would be beneficial for church leaders in geographical proximity to each other to meet more often and design cooperative ministry expansion projects for their area. "Ministry expansion projects" means hard-core church growth strategies, such as training new leaders, finding places for existing and upcoming ministers, multiplying new churches in needy areas, and so on. Some networks, such as the Gulf States Fellowship, based near New Orleans, Louisiana, are already doing this.

5. Recognize and Unleash Mission Structures. Missions is the key to the on-going vitality of the charismatic movement. Without a mission beyond renewal and unity itself, many charismatic groups have already died out. This raises concern about the proportionally small number of missions agencies in major networks of charismatic churches. In some cases, missions agency leaders within networks do not get the same kind of recognition that pastors get.

This bias can be seen in the strong tendency in some circles to brand and snub missions agencies as "parachurch." There is a popular though erroneous notion that missions agencies somehow rank lower than local churches in God's order of things. This is not a matter of semantics, for nothing short of a major shift in theological perspective is needed. We need to recognize that the local church and the missions agency together are peers under the larger umbrella of the church that Christ is building. They serve different but equally important functions in God's redemptive mission.[31]

There is biblical support for this view. Paul's apostolic band launched by the Spirit (Acts 13) models a team of workers whose spiritual gifts converge in a charismatic ministry structure, a Spirit-empowered task force for pioneer evangelism and church planting. This missions structure acted autonomously with respect to the church at Antioch, in much the same way that the Antioch church acted autonomously with respect to the church in Jerusalem. There is no evidence in Scripture that

Paul's missions team was leashed to the Antioch church in the way that many have assumed.[32] More on this later.

In order for networks of charismatic churches to maximize their missionary potential, it will be necessary to create, recognize, and release new kinds of missions structures that work together in cooperative world evangelization efforts. For example, the Gulf States Fellowship has founded its own agency, Gulf States Missions Agency (GSMA), which recruits, equips, and sends out missionaries from the churches within the network. GSMA is also a part of the AIMS network, mentioned earlier. I shall deal with these and other charismatic missions dynamics in the next few chapters.

This chapter illustrates the value of networking on the part of independent charismatic churches. Networking helps eliminate duplication and competition. It allows for maximum local church autonomy without sacrificing ministerial accountability. It preserves unity in diversity. It provides structural cooperation in church growth and world evangelization, but without the bureaucratic overload that stifles growth in many denominations today. That is networking. It works.

NOTES

[1]Bob Mumford, "Don't Miss the Boat," *New Wine*, Vol. 18, No. 1, Jan. 1986, p. 12.

[2]John Naisbitt, *Megatrends: Ten New Directions Transforming Our Lives* (New York: Warner Books, 1984), pp. 211–15ff, 222ff.

[3]Ibid., p. 213 (cf. pp. 212-215).

[4]Ibid., p. 223.

[5]David Barrett, "Statistics, Global," in Stanley M. Burgess and Gary B. McGee, eds., *Dictionary of Pentecostal and Charismatic Movements*, (Grand Rapids: Zondervan, 1988), p. 811.

[6]Lyle E. Schaller, "Reaching a New Generation," *Circuit Rider*, Vol. 10, No. 4, Apr. 1986, p. 109.

[7]John Naisbitt and Patricia Aburdene, *Megatrends 2000* (New York: William Morrow, 1990), p. 291.

[8]E. S. Caldwell quoting Carl George in "Trend Toward Mega Churches," *Charisma*, Aug. 1985.

[9]Barrett, "Statistics, Global," p. 827. My list is a paraphrase of Barrett's and incorporates data from other sources.

[10]Charismatic Bible Ministries brochure/application, May 1987. See also *Network* (Network of Christian Ministries newsletter), Vol. V, No. 7, May/June 1989, p. 2.

[11]Oral Roberts, Charismatic Bible Ministries brochure / application, May 1987.

[12]Ibid.

[13]See Stephen Strang, "Nondenominational Pentecostal and Charismatic Churches," in Burgess and McGee, eds., *Dictionary*, p. 639.

[14]Peter D. Hocken, "Charismatic Movement," in Burgess and McGee, eds., *Dictionary*, p. 141.

[15]Stephen Strang, ed., "Prayer Post Established," *Charisma & Christian Life*, Vol. 14, No. 1, Aug. 1988, p. 20.

[16]Barrett, "Statistics, Global," p. 827.

[17]Hocken, "Charismatic Movement," p. 142.

[18]Bruce Longstreth, ed., "The Year of Equipping the Saints" (Interview), *New Wine*, Vol. 18, No. 1, Jan. 1986, p. 6.

[19]Jean Coleman, "Network of Christian Ministries Meets in Denver," *Ministries*, Vol. 3, No. 5, Fall 1985, pp. 98f.

[20]See Wayne A. Meeks, *The First Urban Christians, the Social World of the Apostle Paul* (New Haven: Yale University Press, 1983), p. 75.

[21]See Walter J. Hollenweger, *The Pentecostals: The Charismatic Movement in the Churches* (Minneapolis: Augsburg, 1972), p. 31, where he quotes and comments on the minutes of the first conference of the Assemblies of God in 1914.

[22]Ibid., pp. 29–30. See also Gary B. McGee, *This Gospel Shall Be Preached* (Springfield, Mo.: Gospel Publishing House, 1989), p. 74. It is interesting that Oral Roberts used this same term, "fraternal fellowship," to describe Charismatic Bible Ministries.

[23]Grant L. McClung, ed., *Azusa Street and Beyond* (South Plainfield, N.J.: Bridge, 1986), pp. 138, 143.

[24]Longstreth, ed., "The Year," p. 6.

[25]Strang, "Nondenominational," p. 639.

[26]Howard Foltz, "Seven Principles for a Pastor in Growing a Missions Church," *Network* (Network of Christian Ministries newsletter), Oct. 1990, p. 1.

[27]Donald A. McGavran, *Momentous Decisions in Missions Today* (Grand Rapids: Baker, 1984), pp. 201ff.

[28]Telephone interview with Network of Christian Ministries administrator, Everett Strong, January 23, 1990.

[29]See C. Peter Wagner, "Church Growth," in Burgess and McGee, eds., *Dictionary*, p. 195.

[30]Bill M. Sullivan, *Creating New Districts in the Church of the Nazarene as a Strategy for Growth* (Pasadena, Calif.: Fuller Theological Seminary, Doctor of Ministry thesis, June 1985), pp. 5, 10–11, 26f.

[31]See Ralph D. Winter, "Two Structures of God's Redemptive Mission," in Ralph D. Winter and Steven C. Hawthorne, eds., *Perspectives on the World Christian Movement* (Pasadena, Calif.: William Carey Library, 1981), p. 178.

[32]See Harold R. Cook, "Who Really Sent the First Missionaries?" *Evangelical Missions Quarterly*, Vol. 11, No. 4, Oct. 1975, p. 233.

A Movement Emerges: Charismatics in Missions

———+———

Chapter 5

A lesson from history, we have noted, is that renewal movements and missionary movements go hand in hand. For example, three of the greatest Catholic missionary orders, the Franciscans, Dominicans, and Jesuits, are products of monastic renewal movements.[1] And the Moravian missionary movement, one of the greatest in Protestant history, was born out of an eighteenth-century Pietistic renewal led by Nicolaus Ludwig von Zinzendorf (1700–1760).[2]

The twentieth-century Pentecostal movement generated one of the greatest missionary movements in all of church history. This awakening began at the turn of the century and almost immediately sent missionaries all over the world. By 1980 there were 180,000 classical Pentecostal churches worldwide comprising some 26 million members. This grew to 320,000 churches and over 45 million members by 1990.[3]

Because of the link between renewal and missions, some have been impatient with the prolonged inward focus of the charismatic movement. John Amstutz posed this challenge in 1985:

> When will the Charismatic movement move from a merely centripetal inward focus on renewal to a centrifugal outward focus on evangelism, especially toward the by-passed hidden "unreached peoples" who account for over fifty percent of the world's population? When will we take seriously the fact that the reason God blesses His people is to make them a blessing (Gen. 12:3) [*sic*].[4]

For a while, it appeared that the charismatic movement would be an exception to the general rule that renewal movements eventually produce missionary movements. Early charismatics in denominations were rightly preoccupied with renewing existing churches. And nondenominational charismatics have had problems of their own.

HINDRANCES TO INDEPENDENT CHARISMATIC MISSIONS

For charismatics staying in denominations, structures for missionary outreach are usually already in place. Here charismatics are now excelling in missions, as we have noted earlier. But independent charismatics, having withdrawn from traditional structures of ministry and missions, are facing a unique set of problems:

1. Structural Limitations. The Protestant Reformation is an example of a renewal movement that was slow to produce a missionary movement. One reason for the delay was that Martin Luther and other reformers rejected the medieval church's only viable missionary structures—the monastic orders.[5] It was not until 1792 that William Carey's famous argument for the "Use of Means for the Conversion of the Heathens" convinced Protestants of the need for missions structures.[6] This led to the founding of the Baptist Missionary Society in 1792. For the next twenty-five years, new Protestant missions agencies multiplied on both sides of the Atlantic, sending missionaries to most parts of the world. The Protestant missionary movement was underway—nearly two centuries after the Reformation.

Analogous to Luther and the other reformers, many independent charismatics rejected traditional approaches to missions and have been slow to come up with functional replacements. Consequently, there are thousands of new independent charismatic churches today without formal ties to organized missions agencies. This is one of the major bottlenecks hindering independent charismatic missions today, according to charismatic missions leader Howard Foltz:

... the vast reservoir of new unaffiliated charismatic churches have no overarching mission structure to facilitate sending thousands of new missionaries from their ranks to the mission field.[7]

2. Strategic Limitations. In a movement so centered on the Holy Spirit, it is not surprising that subjective guidance sometimes preempts objective, researched-based planning. Some years back, for example, a charismatic minister received a "word from the Lord" to evangelize a remote Caribbean island. When he finally reached the island, he found that it had never been inhabited.[8]

Another charismatic leader tried to reach the Muslim world by satellite. He set up a system in the Middle East for transmitting the Gospel in seven Arabic dialects. Until he met missiologist Ralph Winter, however, he did not know that there were 580 Arabic dialects in the region and that only seven percent of the population of the Muslim world speaks Arabic.[9]

These anecdotes underscore the need to balance spiritual guidance and charismatic zeal with informed strategy planning. Current missions data on unreached peoples in virtually all parts of the world are available from the United States Center for World Mission in Pasadena, California, and other research agencies in many cities around the world. The independent charismatic movement does not need to "trust the Lord" to mystically reveal something already researched and documented.

Missions strategy and organization are also urgently needed on the local church level. As Howard Foltz says:

Many [charismatic] churches are not internally organized for missions. They have no missions philosophy or policy statement, no missions committee, do not hold missions conferences and have no plan on how to send out missionaries from their church.[10]

This is not just a problem for charismatics. The Association of Church Missions Committees in Wheaton, Illinois, estimates that less than ten percent of evangelical churches are internally organized for missions.[11] But Foltz is probably right in assuming that charismatic churches rate even lower. Perhaps in our reaction against denominational programs and committees we have thrown out the baby with the bathwater.

3. Inadequate Theology of Mission. The Protestant Reformers adopted a definition of "church" that centered on right doctrine, right teaching, and the right use of the sacraments, with too little emphasis on missionary outreach. In a similar way, charismatics have built new churches around new teachings and spiritual gifts, almost to the exclusion of a sound theology and strategy of missions.

Charismatics inherited little in the way of missions theology from their Pentecostal forebears. It is only in recent decades that Pentecostals have developed their own theology of missions. In many charismatic churches, however, there is little awareness of the biblical basis of missions, and too little emphasis on the Holy Spirit as empowerment for global witness. Even in missions conferences, the preaching and teaching is often out of touch with the discipline of missiology.

What many charismatics *have* inherited from Pentecostalism is a staunch anti-intellectualism. This perpetuates the lack of missions theology. Insisting on homegrown ministry personnel, many churches refuse to send their missionary candidates to the seminary. There are glowing exceptions. For example, Reserve Christian Fellowship in Reserve, Louisiana, helped support me through five years of graduate missiological training at the School of World Mission of Fuller Theological Seminary.

4. Limited Missions Exposure. A recent survey in a missions class of 250 students, mostly independent charismatics, revealed that the majority had never seen a missionary in their home churches. Similar surveys show that most of these students have little or no awareness of global missions concepts, such as Ralph Winter's revolutionary focus on penetrating unreached people groups as the highest priority in missions today.

This lack of missions exposure mirrors the independent churches and leaders. All of this is in stark contrast to many denominational churches where missions is woven into the life of the local church through literature, missions committees, and reports from furloughing missionaries.

In 1986, Howard Foltz discussed these and other bottle-necks that hinder missions mobilization, such as the lack of missionary vision and leadership. Also, a spirit of independence hinders functional unity and cooperation in world evangelization.[12] Foltz and others are convinced that, despite these obstacles, the time has come for the independent charismatic movement to evolve into a worldwide missionary movement.

THE MUST OF WORLD MISSIONS

Assemblies of God missions executive R. B. Cavaness, in a 1986 article, shows how a commitment to missions is often the key to growth and vitality for small churches.[13] Conversely, Pentecostals have also found that a neglect of missions can lead to spiritual stagnation, as Assemblies of God church historian Gary B. McGee observes:

> Spiritual stagnation in local [Assembly of God] churches allegedly resulted from their failure to properly perceive their responsibility for assisting the evangelization of the heathen. . . . In contrast to this condition, churches could be assured of spiritual vitality and growth when actively supporting missions.[14]

Other Pentecostal scholars, such as Donald Gee and Grant McClung, also link the vitality of the Pentecostal movement to its involvement in world missions. But where Pentecostal-charismatic movements have grown inward and ignored the Great Commission, they have consequently slipped into obscurity.[15]

The point is that the health of the independent charismatic

movement is in no small way dependent upon its shift to an outward focus on world evangelization. To repeat the watchword of this book, the Holy Spirit is a missionary Spirit. To frustrate his purpose by using his power and gifts for mere parochial interests is hazardous to the health of the movement.

That is the bad news. The good news is that many charismatics, both denominational and nondenominational, have outgrown a brand of spirituality that sees miracles, healing, and prosperity as ends in themselves. They now see their vast deposit of spiritual and material wealth as a resource for empowering and financing an army of laborers for worldwide evangelism and church planting.

THE MUSCLE FOR WORLD MISSIONS

The charismatics' spiritual heritage richly equips them to meet needs of the unevangelized world. Most of the remaining unreached people groups are found in Third World countries where the supernatural is "natural." In such places, healing by prayer and casting out of demons have played a key role in opening up large segments of the population to the Gospel. For example, Pentecostal-charismatics make up the largest and fastest growing segment of Protestantism in Latin America today. Divine healing, exorcism, and other signs and wonders are among the key factors of growth there, according to C. Peter Wagner.[16] Similarly, a recent doctoral study shows that eighty-one percent of Hindus in India who become Christians do so as a result of the ministry of signs and wonders.[17]

Independent charismatic churches harbor a vast reserve of young people charged with spiritual energy and zeal. The greatest need is for training, mobilization, and financial backing for these potential laborers for world harvest. According to Ralph Winter, only 100,00 new missionaries are needed to complete the task of world evangelization in our generation.[18] Of course they will not all be charismatics, but with some 60,000 independent charismatic churches in the United States alone, there is no reason why the movement cannot supply a large portion of the labor force needed to finish the job.

Funding an army of missionaries is no problem for charismatic churches. Through "seed-faith" they have reaped a surplus of disposable wealth. For example, Fred Price pastors a sixteen-thousand-member independent charismatic church in Los Angeles and teaches the prosperity message. According to C. Peter Wagner, Price has done more to lift blacks from the welfare roles than any other person in Los Angeles.[19] Price founded Crenshaw Christian Center in 1973. Financed by tithes and offerings, the church grew to a $23 million corporation by 1987 with an annual income of $16 million.[20]

This indicates that there is at least some practical value in the prosperity message. The challenge is for charismatic leaders to harness this faith-generated prosperity for world evangelization, something they have barely begun to do. As we have learned from missions researcher David Barrett, Pentecostal-charismatics as a whole give $34 billion a year to general Christian causes, or $1.97 per member per week. But of that amount, only 15 cents per member per week goes to missions or ministry at the world level.[21]

In many ways, charismatic Christianity is uniquely compatible with the cultural settings of the unevangelized world. Divine healing and casting out of demons bring dramatic results in the Third World. In addition to these, the charismatics' practical, need-oriented theology, their emotionally charged worship, and their emphasis on oral expressions, such as speaking in tongues and prophecy, blend right into the cultural landscape of many unreached people groups. Michael Harper, an Anglican charismatic, puts it this way:

> The charismatic renewal does not need to be Africanized; it is African in its very essence. In fact, in another sense, it is "all things to all men." It fits all kinds of spiritualities and culture patterns.[22]

Add to this cultural adaptability the rich spiritual heritage and abundance of human and material resources of the independent charismatic movement. More technology and global information also are currently available than in any previous generation. World travel has never been easier or safer. We have all the resources and means for planting churches in all of the world's twelve thousand currently unreached people groups.

CHARISMATIC MISSIONS EMERGE

Many independent charismatic ministries are already on the cutting edge of the charismatic missionary advance. These trailblazers need to be recognized so that others can follow. The following highlights some exciting developments in charismatic missions over the past four decades.

Pioneers in Charismatic Missions. A prominent figure in the Pentecostal healing revival of the 1950s, T. L. Osborn is considered an independent charismatic missionary pioneer. By the early 1950s, he conducted successful evangelistic campaigns in several countries, reporting scores of miraculous healings and thousands of conversions. By the early 1970s, when the charismatic renewal was nearing its peak, Osborn had already preached the Gospel in some fifty countries, a ministry which was producing over four hundred self-supporting churches per year.[23]

Gordon Lindsay, another leader in the healing revival, crested the mainstream of charismatic renewal through the 1960s. He founded Christ for the Nations Institute (CFNI) in Dallas, Texas, in 1970. Since then, CFNI has served as a major vehicle for training and sending independent charismatic missionaries to various parts of the world. Christ for the Nations, together with its forerunner, the Voice of Healing, has helped build churches for over 8,500 indigenous congregations in seventy-two countries since 1961.[24]

Oral Roberts, America's premier healing revivalist, is one of the most influential figures among independent charismatic ministries today. Founded in 1965, Oral Roberts University (ORU) has become a major training institution for independent charismatics, as well as for students from many denominations. ORU began a "Summer Missions" program in 1976. Summer

Missions annually sends 150 to 200 students into some thirty countries on short-term missions assignments. A typical summer outreach results in tens of thousands of commitments to Christ.[25] Also, combining miracle power and medical science, ORU's "Healing Teams" have tended to health needs in many Third World countries, sharing the Gospel of salvation and the "good news" of preventive health care.[26]

Kenneth E. Hagin, Sr., also a former healing evangelist, withdrew from the Assemblies of God in 1962 and later became a leading faith teacher in the charismatic movement. In 1974 he founded Rhema Bible Training Center, which graduated more than ten thousand students by 1988.[27] Rhema graduates have ministered in every continent of the globe, including communist areas. Rhema's South Africa branch has helped establish more than fifty churches in that nation since 1979.[28]

Osborn, Lindsay, Roberts, Hagin, and a few other leaders of the healing revival, such as Lester Sumrall, rode the crest of the wave into the charismatic renewal and helped launch major missionary advances from their nondenominational charismatic ministries.

Younger-generation charismatics have also pioneered in missions. In 1973, for example, Todd Burke, a twenty-two-year-old graduate of ORU, entered Cambodia in the last days of the Khmer Republic when most foreigners were trying to get out. Through English language classes and a successful evangelistic crusade among the responsive Khmer people, Burke soon gathered a nucleus of young converts and groomed them for church planting. Less than two years later, Burke left behind a network of new churches and leaders, including a four-hundred-member central church in Phnom Penh.[29]

"You can't plant churches in China today," say the experts. But to many missionary-minded charismatics, that sounds more like an invitation than a closed door. For example, Kevin, a young independent charismatic from the United States, recently entered China on a series of tourist visas and planted two underground churches, leaving them to the care of newly trained Chinese pastors.[30]

Charismatic Sending Churches.   Several prominent churches are also contributing to the independent charismatic missionary force. For example, the four-hundred-member Tulsa Christian Fellowship (TCF), the oldest independent charismatic church in Tulsa, Oklahoma, gives about $140,000 a year, thirty percent of its budget, to missions. Forty of TCF's members (a "tithe" of their church) are now serving as overseas missionaries in several countries. On-the-field activities range from Bible translation to pioneer evangelism among unreached people groups.[31]

Larry Stockstill, a young Oral Roberts University gradu- ate, now pastors Bethany World Prayer Center, a four thou- sand-member charismatic church in Baker, Louisiana. Bethany gives more than a million dollars a year to missions—about a third of its annual budget. A total of seventy-two missionaries, working in twenty countries, receive support from Bethany. One-third of these are homegrown missionaries sent out from Stockstill's church.[32]

These examples are merely suggestive of scores of promi- nent charismatic churches making an impact on the world through missions involvement. The successful strategies of these and other sending churches are further analyzed in the next chapter.

Charismatic Sending Agencies.   As in the days of William Carey, independent charismatic groups are now founding their own missions agencies. There are probably several hundred such agencies based in the United States. Prominent examples are:

Calvary Commission, Inc., Lindale, Tex.

Evangel Bible Translators, Rockwall, Tex.

Forward Edge International, Eureka, Calif.

Globe Missionary Evangelism, Pensacola, Fla.

Gulf States Missions Agency, Reserve, La.

India Gospel Outreach, Inc., Alta Loma, Calif.

International Christian Mission, Dallas, Tex.

Missionary Revival Crusade, Laredo, Tex.

New England & World Missions, Worcester, Mass.

Teen Mania Ministries, Tulsa, Okla.

Victory World Mission Outreach, Broken Arrow, Okla.

World Indigenous Missions, New Braunfels, Tex.

These agencies, together with about sixty others, relate together under the Association of International Missions Services (AIMS). AIMS provides a framework for unity and cooperation among charismatic missions agencies so that information and ideas are exchanged and duplication is minimized. Regular newsletters, annual conferences, and other services facilitate this relationship.

These and hundreds of other nondenominational charismatic churches and missions agencies are boldly pioneering new and varied approaches to missionary outreach. In 1984, for example, charismatic leader Dwyatt Gantt organized University Language Services (ULS), which trains and sends English teachers to China as "tentmakers" (cross-cultural witnesses for Christ sent abroad as skilled professionals). With only three weeks of required training and a minimal amount of administrative machinery, candidates are sped on their way. In 1988 alone, ULS had 117 Christians in China teaching English and sharing the love of Christ with their students.

In 1976 a charismatic version of Wycliffe Bible Translators was founded by Syvelle Phillips of Rockwall, Texas. Evangel Bible Translators, as it is called, specializes in training "mother tongue" translators—nationals whose first language is that of the target group. Evangel also mobilizes its translators in evangelism, church planting, and other missionary activities that are usually off limits for Wycliffe translators.

A large number of independent charismatics serve in the Pentecostal-originated sending agency Youth With a Mission (YWAM), which is now independent. Founded by Loren Cunningham in 1960, YWAM has ministered in 215 different countries. Its missionary force consists of 6,000 full-time missionaries and an annual 25,000 short-term missionaries. In addition to YWAM's numbers, there are at least 3,000 career missionaries and 10,000 short-termers per year sent out from independent charismatic churches today, according to Eric Watt, former executive vice president of AIMS.[33] This rivals even the Assemblies of God Foreign Missions Division, which had 1,530 missionaries serving in 120 countries in 1989.[34]

These and other developments support the hypothesis that the independent charismatic church movement is springing forward as the missionary work horse of the charismatic revival. Overall, charismatic missions range from being very effective to being ineffective. The next two chapters offer a representative sampling and analysis of charismatic missionary methods. As the more successful models gain visibility, others can learn from them.

The remaining challenge is to awaken and mobilize tens of thousands of other charismatic churches, ministries, and individuals at large who have not yet been seized by a missionary vision and passion. If charismatic sending churches and missions agencies multiply and tap into this great reservoir of committed personnel, spiritual energy, and material wealth, the independent charismatic church movement will undoubtedly play a major role in bringing about an unprecedented worldwide missionary movement.

NOTES

[1]This statement is not an uncritical endorsement of Roman Catholicism. If it sounds so to Protestant ears, keep in mind that these renewal movements were usually on the periphery of the institutional church, which often suppressed them. The point is that, in monasticism, we find on the one hand genuine attempts to awaken a nominal church, and on the other hand a readiness of these orders (namely the Franciscans, Dominicans, and Jesuits) to send missionaries around the globe to spread their faith to the non-Christian world. See Kenneth Scott Latourette, *A History of Christianity*, Vol. 1 (New York: Harper & Row, 1953, 1975), pp. 427–28.

[2]Kenneth Scott Latourette, *A History of Christianity*, Vol. 2 (New York: Harper & Row, 1953, 1975), p. 897.

[3]David Barrett, "Statistics, Global," in Stanley M. Burgess and

Gary B. McGee, eds., *Dictionary of Pentecostal and Charismatic Movements* (Grand Rapids: Zondervan, 1988), pp. 812–15.

⁴John Amstutz, "Dear Charisma" (letter), *Charisma*, Vol. 11, No. 4, Nov. 1985, p. 7.

⁵Latourette, *A History*, Vol. 2, p. 699.

⁶Ralph D. Winter and Steven C. Hawthorne, eds., *Perspectives on the World Christian Movement* (Pasadena, Calif.: William Carey Library, 1981), p. 227. The editors have excerpted several paragraphs from William Carey's original eighty-seven-page treatise entitled "An Enquiry into the Obligation of Christians to Use Means for the Conversion of the Heathens."

⁷Howard Foltz, "Bottlenecks Hindering Mission Mobilization," *Ministries*, Vol. 4, No. 3, Summer 1986, p. 42.

⁸Ralph Mahoney, "Charting Your Course," *Acts*, Vol. 9, No. 6, Nov./Dec. 1981, p. 2.

⁹Brian Bird, "Reach Every Nation: We Can Do It!" *Ministries*, Vol. 4, No. 3, Summer 1986, p. 30.

¹⁰Foltz, "Bottlenecks," p. 43.

¹¹Ibid.

¹²Ibid., pp. 42–43.

¹³R. B. Cavaness, "A Basic Tenet for Growth in Small Churches," *Ministries*, Vol. 4, No. 3, Summer 1986, p. 32.

¹⁴Gary B. McGee, *This Gospel Shall Be Preached* (Springfield, Mo.: Gospel Publishing House, 1989), p. 100.

¹⁵See Donald Gee, *Spiritual Gifts and the Work of the Ministry Today* (Springfield, Mo.: Gospel Publishing House, 1963), pp. 91ff; cited in L. Grant McClung Jr, ed., *Azusa Street and Beyond* (South Plainfield, N.J.: Bridge Publishing, 1986), p. 141.

¹⁶C. Peter Wagner, *Spiritual Power and Church Growth* (Altamonte Springs, Fla.: Strang Communications, 1986).

¹⁷Larry D. Pate, *From Every People* (Monrovia, Calif.: MARC, 1989), p. 129. The doctoral study on conversions in India is by C. Zechariah. Pate attributes the data to a phone conversation with P.G. Vargis, March 16, 1989.

¹⁸Ralph D. Winter, ed., "The 1990 Unreached Peoples Poster," *Mission Frontiers*, Vol. 11, Nos. 4–5, Apr./May 1989, p. 15.

¹⁹C. Peter Wagner, "Six Crucial Challenges For the Church in the 1990s," *Ministries Today*, Vol. 5, No. 4, July/Aug. 1987, p. 28.

²⁰Paul C. R. Peterson, "An Accurate Picture of Crenshaw Christian Center," unpublished research paper, Pasadena, Calif., Fuller Theological Seminary, May 12, 1987. On p. 10 Peterson quotes Price on these figures.

²¹Barrett, "Statistics, Global," Burgess and McGee, eds., Dictionary, pp. 811, 830, and pp. 814–15 (lines 64, 69).

²²Michael Harper, "Renewal for Mission: an Anglican Perspec-

tive," *International Review of Mission*, Vol. 75, No. 298, Apr. 1986, p. 131.

[23]David Edwin Harrell, Jr., *All Things Are Possible* (Bloomington, Ind.: Indiana University Press, 1975), p. 171.

[24]Christ for the Nations brochure, "Fulfilling the Great Commission in the 80s," n.d. Also confirmed by letter from Larry L. Hill, Missions Director, Christ for the Nations, Inc., July 27, 1990.

[25]Oral Roberts University brochure, "Summer Missions," n.d.

[26]"ORU Medical Missionaries Return With Joyful Reports From All Over The World" (report), *Abundant Life*, Vol 41, No. 4, July/Aug. 1987, pp. 6–10; and Oral Roberts University brochure, "World-Wide Medical Missions," n.d.

[27]Harrell, *All Things are Possible*, p. 186; and Richard M. Riss, "Hagin, Kenneth E.," in Burgess and McGee, eds. *Dictionary*, p. 345.

[28]Kenneth Hagin, Jr., "Trend Toward Faith Movement," *Charisma*, Aug. 1985, pp. 69–70.

[29]John Loftness, "Into All the World," *People of Destiny*, Vol. 4, No. 5, Sept./Oct. 1986, pp. 18–19.

[30]Interview with Kevin, Jan. 15, 1990.

[31]Interview with John W. McVay, Tulsa Christian Fellowship missions administrator, June 23, 1990.

[32]Interview with Rick Zachary, Bethany World Prayer Center missions director, July 3, 1989.

[33]Telephone interview with Eric Watt, Sept. 28, 1989.

[34]Dayton Roberts and John A. Siewert, *Mission Handbook*, 14th ed. (Monrovia, Calif.: MARC; and Grand Rapids: Zondervan, 1989), p. 88. See also Jamie Buckingham, ed., "Insider's Report/News for Ministers," *Ministries Today*, Vol. 7, No. 4, July/Aug. 1989, p. 90.

Charismatic Sending
Churches: A Profile

Chapter 6

An apostolic strategy of the Spirit for independent Charismatic missions! Let us unpack this statement to sample the sentiments of the burgeoning independent charismatic missionary movement. *Apostolic*: Restoring the New Testament pattern according to the charismatic perspective. *Strategy*: Realizing the need for a more informed and structured approach to missions. The *Spirit*: Remaining sensitive to his leading and dependent on his power. *Independent*: Refusing the saddle of a traditional mode. *Charismatic*: Recruiting and releasing missionaries on the basis of spiritual gifts and calling, rather than formal training or position.

These are a few of the overarching dynamics at work in charismatic missions today. But what kinds of charismatic mission structures are replacing the "traditional mode," and how effective are they? Does the "new wheel" spin better than the old one? This chapter and the next describe several different approaches to missions on the part of independent charismatics. Some are analyzed more closely. The aim is to discover the underlying principles and strategies that largely determine the effectiveness of certain models.

CHARISMATIC MISSIONARY MODELS

It is possible to analyze charismatic missions under three basic categories: (1) sending churches, (2) church-related missions structures, and (3) extra-local missions structures. In some situations, these three categories overlap considerably. The latter two categories will be introduced in the next chapter. This chapter will analyze and evaluate charismatic sending churches.

In recent years, many independent charismatic churches

have felt the need to get more directly involved in world missions. Some pastors feel that the local church, rather than the mission agency, is responsible for sending out missionaries. This gives rise to an approach to missions which we shall call the "sending church" model.

SENDING CHURCHES: AN ANALYSIS

"Sending churches" are local congregations that strongly feel that they are to be the sending agent for their missionaries. They may delegate some aspects of missions to extra-local missions agencies, but they do not answer to any higher board, as do some denominational churches. This particular usage of the term "sending church" is maintained throughout this book.

Four Sending Churches. Sending churches are common in charismatic circles, but their efficiency varies. Where they are effective, however, missiological principles usually are being followed, either intuitively or deliberately. Conversely, inefficiency can usually be traced to an unconscious violation of key missiological principles. What follows is an analysis of the proven missions strategies of four well-known charismatic sending churches:

Tulsa Christian Fellowship (TCF), Tulsa, Oklahoma, Bill Sanders, pastor; John McVay, missions administrator.

Victory Christian Center (VCC), Tulsa, Oklahoma, Billy Joe Daugherty, pastor; Dolly Davis, missions director.

Bethany World Prayer Center (BWPC), Baton Rouge, Louisiana, Larry Stockstill, pastor; Rick Zachary, missions pastor.

The Church on the Rock (COTR), Rockwall, Texas, Larry Lea, pastor; David Shibley, missions director (prior to 1990).

In 1990 Larry Lea and David Shibley both relinquished their duties at the Church on the Rock (COTR). Lea now functions in an apostolic relationship to the church as he conducts "Prayer Breakthroughs" around the country; Shibley, with the blessing of the church, founded "Global Advance," a missions organization based in Rockwall, Texas. Apparently, COTR's celebrated missions thrust of the 1980s did not weather this leadership transition very well, at least not initially. But the example set by the church in the past is nevertheless applauded in this chapter as a model for sending churches today.

Table 1 below shows the missions involvement of the four sending churches up to the year 1990.[1] The missionaries do not receive full support from these churches, nor do they all originate from the churches, with the exception of those supported by Tulsa Christian Fellowship (TCF). All but two of these forty missionaries are church members sent out from TCF. In the case of Bethany (BWPC), twenty-two of their missionaries are "homegrown." The rest are "associate" missionaries whose home churches are elsewhere.

FOUR SENDING CHURCHES

Church & Size	Number of Missionaries	Number of Countries	Annual Giving
TCF 400	40	20	$140,000 30% of budget
VCC 8,000	125	50	$480,000 30% of budget
BWPC 4,000	72	20	$1,100,000 33% of budget
COTR* 10,000	40	30	25% of budget

*Prior to changes in 1990.

Figure 2

Success is no accident for sending churches. These key missiological dynamics are at work in all of them. The seven secrets of a healthy sending church, unveiled below, provide models and insights that other churches, even smaller ones, can follow.

1. Leadership. A steadfastly missions-minded senior pastor assisted by a missions director and/or committee (staff or volunteers).

By delegating the leg work of missions to others, the pastors of these and other successful sending churches are free to concentrate on their shepherding responsibilities. Likewise, the missions leaders are relatively free to devote their energies to missions. For example, Mel Cooley, when he served as Church on the Rock's assistant missions director, spent about two-thirds of his time on the field training national leaders. This hands-on involvement with the missionaries in the field usually helps insure that top-level decisions are made from an informed on-the-field perspective.

But a gifted missions director is no substitute for a missions-minded senior pastor who remains steadfastly committed to mobilizing the church in missions. Many zealous missions directors have seen their sprightly proposals bogged in the mire of a senior pastor's "priority" file. Howard Foltz puts it well:

> The senior pastor must take the lead. No church will become a missions church unless the pastor(s) expresses a missions vision. It is one of the pastor's primary responsibilities to educate himself in the Biblical basis of missions and the current needs of the world, pray privately and publicly for missions, and preach missions from the pulpit. He should also seek ways to go on short-term missions trips himself.[2]

2. Resources. A substantially large membership and a financial commitment of at least ten percent of the total budget.

Smaller churches that cannot afford missions staff can learn from the resourcefulness of Tulsa Christian Fellowship (TCF). Comparatively speaking, TCF is a large church, having four hundred members. But it is the smallest of the four sending churches considered here.

A key to TCF's missions success is the mobilization of the laity. Their missions administrator, John McVay, was a volunteer for five years and a part-time staff person for two years before going full-time in 1990. But to take up the slack, the church mobilized a missions task force made up entirely of volunteers. In addition to this, all of the missionaries recruit their own "lay missions agents," people at TCF who act as personal liaisons between the missionaries and church.

Part of the secret is a generous financial commitment. Many charismatic missions leaders agree that ten percent should be a minimum for any church. This commitment should grow as the church grows. For example, in 1985 Pastor Larry Stockstill of Bethany World Prayer Center (BWPC) purposed in faith to graduate their missions giving by $100,000 each year. Their annual giving then was already $500,000. They fulfilled their goal for each year, reaching the one million dollar mark by 1989. To their amazement, the church offerings increased proportionately for each year.

3. Exposure. A strong emphasis on the role of the local church in missions, coupled with consistent missions exposure and promotion.

Healthy sending churches have learned the importance of keeping missions at the center of things. Attractive literature, display boards, regular missions conventions, visiting missionary speakers, and so on, uphold a consistent global missions vision before the people. Regular preaching on missions, especially by the senior pastor, is a vital key.

At Bethany World Prayer Center, for example, annual missions conventions stir the congregation to consistent missions involvement. Bethany's 1975 convention helped inspire my own interest in missions as a career.

In 1977 Tulsa Christian Fellowship launched its missions program with a conference featuring Loren Cunningham, founder of Youth With A Mission. Since then, the annual missions conference has remained the foundation of the missions program. Each conference sees about ninety volunteers for missions service. Of these, perhaps only one or two are sent out as new missionaries each year. But many others are mobilized to greater involvement on the home front through prayer, giving, or serving as a volunteer missions agent.

4. *Training.* Access to a structured ministry and/or missionary training body, such as a local church Bible school or an extra-local training institution.

While charismatics are seldom stymied by their lack of formal education, key missions leaders and missionaries among them are seeing the need for more training. Successful charismatic sending churches, such as those mentioned here, usually require a considerable amount of training for their missions candidates.

For example, Victory Christian Center in Tulsa, Oklahoma, is host to Victory World Missions Training Center (VWMTC). This school was founded by Pastor Billy Joe Daugherty and other charismatic leaders in the Tulsa area. Not to be confused with Victory Bible Institute, VWMTC offers twice yearly a ninety-day intensive training program for mission candidates who have already completed some basic biblical or theological studies. VWMTC offers courses in cross-cultural communications and about fifty other subjects taught by more than fifty veteran ministers and missionaries. The training weighs heavily on the practical side of missions and includes two weeks in another country. Graduates are offered placement opportunities in more than fifty countries and receive various kinds of help in getting to the field. By 1990 more than half of VWMTC's 250 graduates were already serving as missionaries in thirty-nine foreign countries.[3]

Leery of the lay-on-hands-and-go approach to missions, Tulsa Christian Fellowship now encourages a five-stage missionary training program. This includes personal spiritual discipleship, ministry in the home church, cross-cultural exposure, and biblical, theological, and missiological studies. An added boost to TCF missions is the fact that about half of their people have had some theological training at nearby Oral Roberts University. A similar pattern has been observed at the Church on the Rock in Rockwall, Texas, where several of their missionary candidates received training and missions exposure at Christ for the Nations Institute in nearby Dallas.

5. *Structure.* Relationships with certain types of established missions structures which serve the missionaries in various ways.

Each of the four churches considers itself the sending authority for missionaries. However, their missions leaders are ready to admit that the local church cannot be a full-fledged missions agency. John McVay, for example, sees Tulsa Christian Fellowship's relationship to extra-local organizations as the ideal. He says,

> We tried to be a mission agency. I have had missionaries in different parts of the world that have wanted our church to be their mission agency. But we've got our hands full being a sending church. Missionaries need and deserve the encouragement that a mission agency on their field can provide.[4]

Realizing the ineffectiveness of the "church-equals-the-missions-agency" model, Tulsa Christian Fellowship now sends its missionaries out under established missions organizations, such as Wycliffe Bible Translators, Youth With A Mission, and University Language Services, a charismatic group that sends English teachers to China.

Before the 1990 leadership transition, the Church on the Rock had one of the largest local church missions programs in the United States. David Shibley, its missions director during the 1980s, agrees that a missionary needs both a sending church and a service agency. "I don't believe that God requires the local church to be linguistic experts or to have the capacity to teach cultural anthropology," says Shibley.[5] Like Tulsa Christian Fellowship, COTR espoused the concept of linking its missionaries with established service agencies.

Similarly, Victory Christian Center has nonbureaucratic ties to three charismatic missions agencies which help service and maintain their missionaries on the field. And in Baton

Rouge, Louisiana, Bethany World Prayer Center also strongly encourages its missionaries to work through some type of missions organization, such as the Gulf States Missions Agency based near New Orleans.

6. Contacts. Relationships with apostolic ministries on the field.

If you were to inquire of these sending churches as to who directs the activities of the charismatic missionary, the Holy Spirit would be at the head of the list. But even under the Spirit, practical direction is provided through a spontaneous interplay within the sending church, the missions agency, and the "apostolic" ministries (missionaries or indigenous workers) on the field where the missionary serves. Here is how it usually works.

Sending churches, including the ones analyzed here, expect their missionaries to carry on the "vision of the house," or the spirit or flavor of their congregational ministry. Also, these churches maintain a close pastoral relationship with their missionaries, especially in their early years on the field. But these and other successful charismatic sending churches do not short-leash their missionaries. While field selection and placement is usually a joint venture by the sending church and the missions agency, it is primarily the missionary who, under the leading of the Spirit, decides where he or she wants to serve. Likewise, missions strategy is largely up to the missionary. This is where apostolic ministries on the field play a key role.

Strong charismatic sending churches have close relationships with senior missionaries and indigenous apostolic ministries in various parts of the world. Younger missionaries are usually encouraged to work under the direction and supervision of these senior ministers. As they mature, however, a partnership may develop, or they may start their own work on the field. They are then in a key position to help train younger missionaries.

The above pattern is typical in charismatic missions. It provides an effective model for mobilizing missionaries in a structure that maintains a delicate balance between missionary autonomy and accountability under the guidance of the Holy Spirit.

7. *Pastoral Care.* Some means for providing on-going pastoral care for missionaries on the field.

According to Gordon White, veteran missionary to Africa, the key to a healthy missions force is pastoral care. However, the lack of pastoral care was shown to be the cause of considerable or extreme stress to thirty-five percent of the missionaries who responded to a 1983 survey, according to White.[6] How do charismatic sending churches care for their missionaries?

At Tulsa Christian Fellowship, lay "missions agents" maintain contact with their missionaries, representing their needs to the congregation. This not only benefits the missionaries, but it is also a vital key to the life of the church, according to TCF missions administrator, John McVay.

"We feel that the responsibility of the local church is to care for missionaries," says David Shibley, former missions director at the Church on the Rock.[7] As missions pastor, it was Shibley's policy not to surrender pastoral care for the church's missionaries to extra-local missions agencies. Shibley and other COTR ministers pastored the missionaries through personal visits on the field whenever possible. They also linked individual missionaries to specific home cell groups at COTR. Care group leaders mobilized the cells in letter-writing and prayer for the missionaries assigned to them.

Bethany World Prayer Center has also maintained warm pastoral relationships with their missionaries. When counsel or advice is needed, the missionary may call collect any time and from any place. In the event of a severe crisis, Bethany's missions pastor pledges a personal visit to the missionary as soon as possible.[8] The Center's missionary trainees are held directly accountable to the leadership of the church, especially during the first four years from recruitment. The purpose is not to control or dominate, but to nurture and develop the missionaries on a personal level. The result is a stronger, healthier missions force. As missionaries mature in ministry and in their relationships to other senior missionaries on the field, they are given more freedom to pursue their own vision and goals.

These four charismatic sending churches have been analyzed because of their high visibility among charismatics. This is not intended to diminish the importance of many other charismatic sending churches. For example, Reserve Christian Fellowship, in Reserve, Louisiana, gives about $120,000 in annual support of some twenty-five missionary couples and five singles in more than a dozen countries, including the United States.

The age, size, prominence, and international savvy of the churches examined above are crucial to their success. But their success stories are not typical of *all* charismatic churches trying to be the sending agent for their missionaries.

SENDING CHURCHES: AN EVALUATION

Generally, churches trying to be full-fledged missions agencies are not very effective. This is true not only of charismatic churches but of noncharismatic churches as well. For example, the movement known as the Churches of Christ believes it is illegitimate for local churches to delegate aspects of missions to extra-local organizations. However, an evaluation by Philip W. Elkins has shown that most of these churches fell short of this ideal during a ten-year diagnostic period. Elkins found that where these churches were effective in missions, extra-local entities had crept in to assist the churches in training, mobilizing, and supervising their missionaries.[9]

Our analysis of successful charismatic sending churches is consistent with Elkins' findings. The success of our four model churches has depended upon relying on extra-local organizations for help in training, servicing, and supervising their missionaries. Unfortunately, effective sending churches are in the minority. Not all attempts to be the sending agent are accompanied with the same degree of success. Yet, like the Churches of Christ, many charismatic churches still insist on managing the missionary task single-handedly.

Weaknesses of the Sending Church Model. On-the-field supervision of missionaries is a proven key to effective missions. Most churches cannot provide that supervision without the help of extra-local bodies. Many charismatic churches claiming to be the missions agency are simply pumping money into the hands of "lone ranger" missionaries who are not really accountable to anyone. For example, Pastor Ken Sumrall of Liberty Church in Pensacola, Florida, found this to be true of his own church in earlier years. A visit to the field opened his eyes to the problem. This moved him to found Globe Missionary Evangelism (GME) in April 1973,[10] now one of the premier charismatic missions sending agencies.

Another tendency is for large, influential charismatic churches to send only missionaries whom, or support only works, which they themselves can control. This is a problem, especially where local church missions leaders are not missiologically informed. Jim Zirkle, a prominent charismatic missions leader, is well acquainted with this problem:

> I deal with "appointed" missionary directors all the time. To be frank, most of them are just hirelings on someone's payroll. They've never slept in the dirt or pushed away an animal they didn't want in bed with them. If you are going to be a missions director, you have to understand what missions is all about. . . . If you have someone to represent you in missions, at least send them out to the field for a season to see what it's all about.[11]

Generally speaking, most local church leaders are not in a position to plan the strategy and control the affairs of an overseas ministry. Furthermore, this approach is not biblical. Contrary to prevailing notions in some quarters, it cannot be shown from Scripture that Paul the apostle and his mission team were directed or supervised by the church at Antioch, even though the team launched out from that congregation.[12] Called forth and commissioned by the Spirit, the apostolic company was an extra-local entity, having as much authority and autonomy as any local church. The team itself had authority over churches it planted, as Paul's letters show. Those new churches were not branches of the Antioch church. This calls into question the efforts of charismatic churches to control overseas missions and ministries.

Another prevailing trend is for charismatic churches to substitute missions trips for missions. A typical pattern is for the pastor and perhaps a few others from the church to visit a missions point for several days, participating in various types of evangelism or church nurture, usually through language translators. They may evangelize in crusades or in churches, or address groups of pastors, and so on, leaving behind little or no visible evidence of church growth. And they tend to repeat the same processes year after year, without evaluating their effectiveness.[13]

Such missions trips are extremely helpful for investigating works or sparking a global vision in the local church. But to many charismatic churches, this *is* missions—this is the extent of their involvement. This raises serious questions with regard to financial stewardship, as Zirkle observes:

> In the end the money that is supposed to be invested in missions has been used up. They didn't invest in missions. . . . They invested in themselves instead. All that was accomplished was a bunch of little glory trips[14]

Other weaknesses attend the charismatic sending church model.[15] Some churches send out missionaries who lack training and are unprepared to deal with cultural differences. Others expect their *charismata* (spiritual gifts) to accomplish the entire missionary task. Practical administrational dynamics are largely ignored. Duplication, or lack of cooperation with other charismatic missionaries working in the same area is another problem. Related to this is the lack of a strategic approach to field selection on the part of many churches.

Perhaps the knottiest problem with the sending church model is an intrinsic one, that is, the ever-lurking possibility of a gradual or sudden shift in priority or philosophy of missions on the part of the sending church. This has happened in charismatic churches, large and small. Missionaries have had to come home and look elsewhere for support. Some have never returned to the field. For example, only three or four of the forty missionaries supported by the Church on the Rock before 1990 remained on the roll shortly after the transition mentioned earlier in this chapter.

Given the pitfalls, is the sending church model worthy of emulation? I believe it is, especially where issues and cautions like those represented here are taken seriously. What generally determines the ultimate success of the sending church is whether or not the leaders are willing to delegate significant aspects of missions to entities outside of their own four walls. The church that tries to expedite every aspect of the missionary task is usually ineffective, not to mention unbiblical. This is the verdict of the historical record, as missions scholar Harold R. Cook observes:

> . . .we do not read our history carefully and realize that when the church has brought [missions] under control, it has tended to stifle rather than stimulate the work. At best, as in the council at Jerusalem, it tags along behind and grudgingly acknowledges what the Spirit is doing.[16]

On the other hand, sending churches willing to cooperate with each other and with various types of organizations not tied to one local church are enjoying a meaningful measure of success.

Strengths of the Sending Church Model. Successful sending churches exhibit a number of strengths. First, this model emphasizes the centrality of the Holy Spirit and the local church in world evangelization. This produces a breed of homegrown missionaries whose primary orientation and source of ministerial identity is the local church, not the seminary or missions agency. Consequently, many charismatics contribute to planting and strengthening local churches as a matter of course, even though church planting as such may not be stressed.[17]

Second, this model diminishes the church-versus-missions dichotomy that exists in some streams of evangelicalism.

Churches become more practically involved in ministry on the world level. This gives them a real taste of the church's "sentness," thus filling a spiritual need that is basic to every local church—the need to be actively engaged in God's redemptive mission on earth. As pioneer missiologist Roland Allen puts it, ". . .the church which does not conquer the world dies."[18] In the final analysis, the church at Antioch needed Paul as much as he needed them, because they needed to be a vital part of God's mission to the world.

Third, the sending church model allows for the rapid deployment of a vast supply of resources to meet new global challenges and opportunities. This is particularly true of independent charismatic churches which, as we have repeatedly noted, make up the fastest growing religious movement in America today.[19] There is no shortage of willing and available personnel in this movement. It is not unusual to witness a hundred people volunteering for missionary service at a charismatic missions conference. Also, the emphasis on God's abundant provision has placed a vast supply of disposable wealth in the hands of giving Christians. As charismatics learn the "why" of prosperity in terms of global missions, billions of dollars will be released for the cause.

The factors contributing to the success of the sending churches analyzed here can be adapted and applied to smaller churches, through cooperation with area sister churches and links to established missions organizations. Many charismatic churches today are multiplying their efficiency by banding together in cooperative missions efforts.

An encouragement to smaller churches, Tulsa Christian Fellowship demonstrates that lay missions leaders can be effective. Though quality may sometimes lag in the ranks of volunteers, it often excels. People are mobilized in a cause bigger than life itself.

In this chapter, we have analyzed and evaluated one particular model of independent charismatic missions—the sending church. The sending church sees itself as the sending agent for its missionaries but recognizes the need to cooperate with extra-local structures. Other charismatic models were mentioned, and the need for smaller churches to cooperate with one another and with missions organizations was stressed. These issues are further addressed in later chapters.

Finally, as mentioned earlier, much of what contributes to the success of the four sending churches studied in this chapter can be duplicated in smaller charismatic churches. The real key is not resources, but resourcefulness; not the size of the congregation, but the size of the church's vision. Where smallness exists as a mind-set, it becomes a major hindrance to global harvest, but small churches with a large vision can become an effective force for world evangelization.

NOTES

[1]The data for this chart and for much of this book was collected through interviews and correspondence with the missions leaders of each of these four churches in 1989 and 1990. Another primary source for the same empirical data is the promotional literature produced by these churches (pamphlets, brochures, etc.).

[2]Howard Foltz, "Seven Principles for a Pastor in Growing a Missions Church," *Network* (Network of Christian Ministries newsletter), Oct. 1990, p. 1.

[3]Interview with Dolly Davis, missions director at Victory Christian Center, January 12, 1990. Letter from Davis, August 17, 1990.

[4]Interview with McVay, June 23, 1989. Letter from McVay, July 30, 1990.

[5]Interview with Shibley, February 25, 1989.

[6]Gordon White, "Pastoral Counseling—the Key to a Healthy Mission Force," *Evangelical Missions Quarterly*, Vol. 25, No. 3, July 1989, pp. 304ff.

[7]Interview with Shibley, February 25, 1989.

[8]Larry Stockstill and Rick Zachary, *Bethany World Prayer Center Missions Policy Manual*(Baker, La.: unpublished, n.d.), pp. 21, 38.

[9]Philip Wayne Elkins, *Church-Sponsored Missions: An Evaluation of Churches of Christ*, (Austin, Tex.: Firm Foundation Publishing House, 1974), pp. 25–56.

[10]Michele Buckingham, "Retaining the Excitement That Motivates Missions," *Ministries*, Vol. 4, No. 3, Summer 1986, p. 45.

[11]See Jim Zirkle, *Missions: The How To, Part IV—Standards*(Tulsa, Okla.: Jim Zirkle, n.d.), p. 13.

[12]See Harold R. Cook, "Who Really Sent the First Missionaries?" *Evangelical Missions Quarterly*, Vol. 11, No. 4, Oct. 1975, p. 233.

Refuting the common notion that the Antioch church was a missionary "sending church" or "sending agency," Cook advances the following arguments (this is a paraphrased summary): (1) The Antioch church as such was not involved in the sending of Barnabas and Saul. There is no evidence that the leaders involved were acting on behalf of the church. (2) These leaders simply "released" (*apoluo*, Acts 13:3) the missionaries in response to the Spirit's prompting. It was the Spirit who "sent" (*pempo*, v. 4) them. (3) Paul and Barnabas were not "accountable" to the Antioch church as such. In Acts 14:27 the return visit and report was initiated by the missionaries, not required by the church. (4) Beyond Acts 13 there is no record of further missionary activity on the part of the Antioch church. This makes untenable the argument that this church constituted a missionary sending agency. (5) The Antioch church was not structurally equipped to act as a missionary sending agency. (6) It is the Holy Spirit who sent and directed the missionaries from Antioch, just as he had sent Philip to the Ethiopian in Acts 8:29, and Peter to Cornelius in Acts 11:12.

[13]That these are major trends is documented through interviews with charismatic scholars and leaders, some of whom prefer to remain anonymous. Some of the information is based on questionnaires filled out by large numbers of charismatics from virtually every state in the United States.

[14]Zirkle, *Missions: The How To*, p. 14.

[15]For a summary of comparable strengths and weaknesses on the part of the Churches of Christ sending churches, see Elkins, *Church-Sponsored Missions*, pp. 49, 83.

[16]Cook, "Who Really Sent?" p. 239.

[17]See David Shibley, *A Force in the Earth*, (Altamonte Springs, Fla.: Creation House, 1989), p. 141.

[18]Roland Allen, *Missionary Principles*, (Grand Rapids: Eerdmans, 1964), p. 144.

[19]C. Peter Wagner, "Church Growth," *Dictionary of Pentecostal and Charismatic Movements*, Stanley M. Burgess and Gary B. McGee, eds., (Grand Rapids: Zondervan, 1988), p. 192.

Charismatic Missions Agencies: Creating New Patterns for World Evangelization

———+———

Chapter 7

One idea that has been central to our argument is that renewal movements often give birth to new structures for missionary outreach. The Waldensians and the Lollards of the Medieval period, and the Pietists and the Methodists of the seventeenth and eighteenth centuries are examples of renewed Christians forging new missions strategies for penetrating various segments of the unchurched world. The charismatic renewal is consistent with this historical pattern. Both denominational and independent charismatics are on the forefront of a new missionary thrust. And the independent charismatic movement is generating what is possibly the strongest and most consistent missionary drive of the renewal.[1]

Independent charismatics are busily pioneering their own structures and strategies for missionary outreach. The charismatic "sending church" described in an earlier chapter is one approach. This chapter examines a variety of charismatic missions structures (see Figure 3).

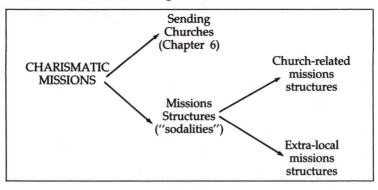

Figure 3

In the discipline of missiology, "missions structures" are called "sodalities" because they specialize in recruiting and mobilizing committed workers beyond local church ("modality") involvement to task-oriented, cross-cultural missionary outreach. This meaning of the term "missions structure" or "missions agency" is used for the remainder of this book.[2]

Some charismatic missions structures operate more or less under the auspices of local churches (see Figure 4). For convenience, we will call these *church-related* missions structures. Analyzed below, missions structures of this type are related to a church or a group of churches that provide varying degrees of pastoral oversight and financial subsidy.

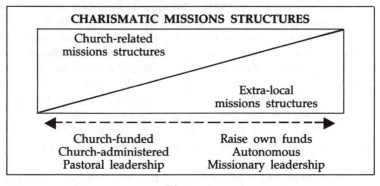

Figure 4

But as you move to the right of the spectrum (Figure 4), missions structures are increasingly *extra-local* in nature. That is, the churches lead less and less and the missionaries lead more and more. And in some cases, these extra-local missions structures raise their own funds from a broad pool of churches and individual donors. The second part of this chapter describes a variety of extra-local missions structures.

Charismatic missionaries usually receive ordination in their home churches. Individual missionaries in virtually all types of charismatic missions are expected to raise their own support, since "living by faith" is central to the charismatic value system.

CHURCH-RELATED MISSIONS STRUCTURES

Victory World Missions Training Center, described in chapter 6, is an example of a church-related missions structure. As we saw in chapter 4, some of the newly-formed networks of independent charismatic ministries are starting their own missions programs for sending out and serving missionaries from their churches. Examples of these include the Gulf States Missions Agency and Faith Christian Fellowship International, led by Doyle (Buddy) Harrison in Tulsa, Oklahoma.

Formed in 1978, Faith Christian Fellowship represents about one thousand ordained ministers and some three hundred charismatic churches. They have a missionary support office in Newark, Delaware, which helps their churches with the administrative side of missions. But the missionaries are accountable to their sending churches, which are usually their training ground. The support office has helped launch twenty-four missionaries who are now serving in some fifteen countries. Churches and Bible schools have been established or "adopted" in Africa, Asia, Europe, and Latin America.[3]

Gulf States Missions Agency. The Gulf States Missions Agency, based in Reserve, Louisiana, is an independent charismatic, church-related missions agency. It was formed in 1986 by Rod Aguillard, Dick Bashta, I, and other pastors belonging to the Gulf States Pastors Fellowship, a network of independent charismatic leaders representing nearly two hundred churches, mainly in the deep South. Gulf States Missions coordinates a five-stage process for recruiting, training, sending, and supervising missionaries from churches in the Gulf States Pastors' Fellowship.[4] This is an apprentice model, centered in the concept of the local church. Virtually all of the board members of Gulf States Missions are senior pastors of area local churches.

By the end of 1990, after only four years' existence, Gulf

States Missions had already commissioned fifteen new missionary couples and nine new single missionaries into cross-cultural ministry in eight countries outside of the United States. The mission also backs several other established missionaries in various parts of the world. They emphasize evangelism, church planting, and leadership training among unreached people groups.

Given their solidarity with local churches, Gulf States Missions and other church-related charismatic missions are tapping into a rich supply of resources for world evangelization—the finances, the available personnel, and most of all, an army of prayer warriors who know how to pray for local and global harvest. But one of the greatest strengths of church-related missions lies in what they do for the churches. The missions input makes them feel part of a world-class movement that combines local interests with global concerns. It mobilizes them in prayer and giving. It empowers "ordinary" members to move from their pews into active, full-time involvement in the harvest among unchurched peoples of the world.

Living Water Teaching. One example of this involvement is Living Water Teaching Missions, based in Tulsa, Oklahoma. Jim Zirkle founded this mission in 1979. A year or so later, his brother Jerry founded Living Water Teaching Church, which became the administrative and support base for the mission. During the decade of the eighties, more than two hundred members of Jerry's church were trained and launched into full-time ministry through the Living Water Teaching Missions, though not all have continued to work with this mission. Living Water Teaching Missions and Living Water Teaching Church, then, are seen as a unit, the mission being the outreach arm of the local church. Yet, in contrast to Gulf States Missions Agency, the mission is mainly led by hands-on, field-wise missionaries and missions leaders.

Living Water Teaching also recruits missionary trainees from other sending churches. In the late 1980s it had more than 120 workers on the field. Some of these have joined or started other ministries. Living Water Teaching currently has about ninety missionaries serving in six countries, mainly in Central America. During the 1980s, more than forty thousand recorded conversions were attributed to the labors of Living Water Teaching. Its basic strategy is to set up Bible schools for training national leaders who in turn evangelize, plant churches, or nurture existing churches. Even though church planting is not stressed as a component of its strategy, some Living Water Teaching workers have actually multiplied large families of indigenous churches.[5]

Church-Related Missions: An Appraisal.   What makes Living Water Teaching, Gulf States Missions Agency, and other church-related missions tick? First of all, in church-centered missions no one is sent out without first proving himself or herself in the context of a local church ministry. Gulf States missionaries, for example, generally know their spiritual gifts and how to use them responsibly. They understand basic principles of Christian living, church government, pastoral authority, prayer, and spiritual warfare. Most of all, they know how to lead people to Christ, teach them basic Bible truths, and ground them in a solid local church. Anything short of that is not effective evangelism.

Second, these missions structures are producing a generation of church-centered missionaries. The local church is their training ground. Many of them have no seminary or para-church training. They are often prejudiced against para-church ministries that do not contribute directly to the multiplication and nurture of local churches. Their leaders are pastors who have instilled in them the idea that the local church is the most effective tool of evangelism. Consequently, these missionaries intuitively know the value of planting or strengthening local churches on the field.

Apprenticeship training for missionaries also adds strength to this model. It begins in the home church, under the pastor, and is extended to the field with the help of a senior missionary. It requires no formal education, but it does help to dispel the myth among some charismatics that spiritual gifts and the laying on of hands are all that one needs to become an effective missionary.

For example, Gulf States Missions Agency's training model takes anywhere from three to five years. This includes nine months of intensive Bible and missions training in a classroom setting. The rest of the training involves apprenticeship under senior ministers. "Graduation" for a trainee means becoming the leader of a major mission work or pioneering a new work, and being able to help train, mobilize, and supervise a team of budding apprentices for Gulf States Missions.

A potential weakness threatens church-related missions, however. In some cases, leaders lack knowledge and experience in cross-cultural missions. A creative solution to this problem is the mission agencies' links to senior missionaries and indigenous pastors in various parts of the world. These senior ministers take apprentices under their wings, provide supervision and evaluation, and insure accountability. Major problems are often referred to the missionary's senior pastor and sending church.

A major danger for church-based missions is the historically recurring process by which churchly structures gradually absorb mission structures which then lose their missionary edge, turning instead to churchly and pastoral concerns, sometimes in the name of "home missions." This is what missiologist C. Peter Wagner calls "The Babylonian Captivity of the Christian Mission."[6]

EXTRA-LOCAL MISSIONS STRUCTURES

In contrast to church-related missions, some charismatic missions agencies are "extra-local" or "trans-local" in structure and authority. These are not as closely tied to any one local church or group of churches. Church-related missions and extra-local missions are on either end of a spectrum with a variety of agencies in between (see Figure 5).

Youth With A Mission is an example of a trans-local missions structure that is not tied to any one church or denomination. On the left end of the spectrum, Gulf States

Missions Agency, as we have seen, is administered by pastors. Somewhere near the center of the spectrum, the nondenominational charismatic group known as the People of Destiny International (PDI) is led by an "apostolic team" which is spiritually related to the churches of that movement. These churches contribute to an "apostolic team fund" to help support the endeavors of the team. The apostolic team, however, is a mobile, trans-local ministry structure, clearly and conscientiously distinguished from local church leadership.

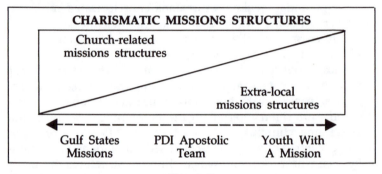

Figure 5

Let us survey five major types of extra-local charismatic mission structures with a closer look at this exciting innovation, the mobile apostolic team.

1. Apostolic Teams. In 1986 charismatic teacher Derek Prince, then seventy-one years of age, made this statement while reflecting on main areas of overlooked biblical truths to be recaptured and restored to the twentieth-century church: "I've also begun to see that in a certain sense the major outreach arm of the Church should be apostolic teams."[7]

An apostolic team, as understood by some charismatics, is a band of spiritually gifted, spiritually related, proven leaders who facilitate the planting and/or nurture of churches and the training and ordaining of leadership in those churches. Like

Paul's apostolic team in Acts, these teams are mobile and not under the control of their sending churches.

New Covenant Commission. As mentioned in chapter 5, Todd Burke's church-planting venture in Cambodia (now Kampuchea) was largely accomplished through the apostolic team approach in embryo. After his ministry in Cambodia and other Asian nations, Burke formed the New Covenant Commission, which was later dissolved. During much of the 1980s, however, the New Covenant Commission used the apostolic team approach in evangelism, leadership training, and church planting in the United States and in cross-cultural settings around the world.[8]

People of Destiny International. In 1982 Larry Tomczak and C. J. Mahaney founded People of Destiny International for the purpose of establishing local churches and training leaders. No other charismatic group has given more definition and focus to the apostolic team approach than People of Destiny. Tomczak leads a mobile apostolic team of four to six men. In this movement, local church leadership and the apostolic team are two distinct, semiautonomous entities of church government. The team members all belong to local churches. However, their authority is not derived from the churches, but from the Holy Spirit through charismatic gifts such as those listed in Ephesians 4:11—the so-called five-fold ministry gifts (apostle, prophet, evangelist, pastor, and teacher). The team's association with the sending churches is spiritual and relational. A sending church releases and commends apostolic team members to their work. It does not command them.

The main function of the apostolic team is to raise up new churches, train and appoint leaders in those churches, and then help facilitate the healthy growth and development of the churches. The team trains and mobilizes church planters to help carry out this function. In some cases, the team "adopts" existing churches. Churches planted or nurtured by the team are not legally tied to each other, but their submission to the team's authority is Spirit-born and voluntary.

This creative adaptation of the classic Pauline method is vindicated by its fruits. The movement began in 1979. By 1989 People of Destiny had planted nineteen new churches in the United States, one in the Philippines, and one in Mexico. The average size of these churches is about three hundred, counting only those persons who have completed a ten-to-twelve-week new members' class. That is a total of six thousand committed Christians gathered over a single decade. Although most of People of Destiny's church planting has not been cross-cultural, its apostolic team model is an effective missions structure that has been used successfully abroad. The church plans to send more teams to plant churches in other countries.[9]

Many leading missiologists agree that the dynamics of the apostolic teams in the book of Acts display ideal principles for all true missionary structures. Authority and leadership patterns are charismatic, not legal or hierarchical. Bureaucracy is minimal. The Spirit, not the church, is the ultimate sending authority. The teams are equal partners with local churches but are never controlled or absorbed by them. The teams stay mobile as they plant, nurture, and doctor churches and train new leaders both for the pastorate and for the apostolate.[10]

People of Destiny International, along with other charismatic groups, seem to be recapturing some of these pristine dynamics of the first-century apostolic teams.[11] All mission structures, regardless of their organizational form, should contend for these ideals, maintaining the apostolic function of leading people to Christ through church planting, church nurture, and leadership training. For this cause mission structures exist. To drift from the apostolic function to what C. Peter Wagner calls "the syndrome of church development" is to forfeit their right to exist.[12]

Turning now to other types of extra-local charismatic mission structures, it is important to keep the above ideals in mind. Although the structures vary, virtually all charismatic mission leaders espouse the Pauline model and the book of Acts as their standard for missionary outreach.

2. Training / Sending Agencies. Many charismatic missions agencies look much like traditional Protestant missionary societies, conforming to what some call the "para-church" model. They recruit and train missionary candidates from a variety of churches, sending them out under varying degrees of directive supervision. Some examples given previously include Youth With A Mission, Globe Missionary Evangelism, and Christ for the Nations International.

Youth With A Mission. We have already looked at Youth With A Mission (YWAM) in some detail. We noted that, while this group is multidenominational (as over against independent charismatic), they have more independent charismatic missionaries than any other agency. In many ways, YWAM serves as the key model for emerging charismatic sending agencies. They have an efficient training program with a Christian university in Hawaii and 143 Discipleship Training Schools around the world.

YWAM has specialized in short-term missions, sending out some 25,000 volunteers each summer. In one particular year, they had over 100,000 short-term participants. But during the 1980s they began emphasizing the long term, setting a goal for 50,000 full-time workers and making specific plans for multiplying indigenous churches among major blocks of the world's unreached people groups. Their "Target 2000" proposal of 1988 includes a goal to send pioneering teams to 450 world-class cities by the year 2000.[13]

YWAM is distinguished in missions history because of its international character. Several leading missiologists have begun to see Third World missions as the wave of the future for world evangelization. By the year 2000, based on current growth rates, more than half of all Protestant missionaries will be from the Third World.[14] But as early as 1990, non-Westerners already made up thirty-two percent of all YWAMers, and the leaders aim to increase this to sixty percent by the end of the 1990s.

YWAM's founding president, Loren Cunningham, says, "As I see the world today, some of the greatest potential for missions is third-world people. They're a huge, untapped area."[15] By 1989, YWAM had already begun forming partnerships with Third World mission agencies, setting new patterns for a new era of world evangelization.[16] Being one of the largest missionary sending agencies in the world, these factors make YWAM a major force for global harvest, especially considering the fact that church planting is now a pivotal part of their strategy.

Globe Missionary Evangelism. Globe Missionary Evangelism was founded in 1973 by Ken Sumrall, pastor of Liberty Church, a large independent charismatic congregation in Pensacola, Florida. Globe raises support from churches and individuals across the country. They are not dependent on any one group. Globe's leaders stress the need for a separate mission structure for sending, serving, and supervising missionaries. Workers are accountable to the mission, which appoints field directors in areas where multiple families serve. If there is a major problem with a missionary, Globe may consult that person's sending church, but the mission is the final authority.

As needed, Globe missionaries receive training from Liberty Christian College, also founded by Ken Sumrall and located in Pensacola, Florida. The college offers a Bachelor of Missions degree, and most of Globe's missionaries are graduates of Liberty Christian College.

Globe maintains six single missionaries and fifty-two missionary families serving in twenty-one countries around the world. With many of the wives active in ministry, this is no small missionary force. Activities include evangelism, church planting, founding and/or teaching in Bible schools, or helping existing churches. The missionaries receive all the administrative backing and legal covering one would expect of a well-established mission.[17]

World Indigenous Missions. Founded in the late 1970s, World Indigenous Missions is an independent charismatic training and sending agency based in New Braunfels, Texas.

This mission stresses close relationships with local churches, but it is funded almost entirely by the missionaries. Virtually all of its leaders are experienced missionaries who are currently active in cross-cultural ministry. Even the president, Steve Johnson, is a hands-on, cross-cultural missionary. This gives the mission's policy-setters and decision-makers the insights and experience needed to guide the mission along the right track.

World Indigenous Missions uses a well-developed apprentice model for training missionaries in cross-cultural settings. It begins with nine months of missions education and language and culture learning. Next, the recruit is apprenticed to a senior missionary on the field for one year. After that, the new missionary may continue to serve in that post, or launch out in pioneer church planting under the supervision of the senior missionary. Specializing in church planting and leadership training, World Indigenous Missions has sixty missionaries serving in seven countries, including Mexico, France, Germany, Spain, and the Philippines.[18]

These organizations represent scores of new charismatic sending agencies currently mobilizing thousands of independent charismatic missionaries who would probably not feel comfortable in traditional missionary societies.

3. Charismatic Service Agencies. "Would you take care of our business affairs when we go to the foreign field?" This request from missionary friends of Gary Rechtfertig of Tulsa, Oklahoma, moved him to organize Victory World Missions Outreach in 1985.[19] Not to be confused with Victory World Missions Training Center or Victory Christian Center (chapter 6), Victory World Missions Outreach is a premier example of a nondirective charismatic mission *service* agency, bridging the gap between sending churches and the foreign field.

The primary difference between a sending agency and a service agency has to do with the locus of authority. A sending agency sets requirements for its missionaries and has authority over them. A service agency, in contrast, conscientiously leaves that authority in the hands of the sending church and the receiving church or local ministry where the missionary serves. Therefore, this places service agencies somewhere near the center of the *church-related/extra-local* spectrum (Figure 4). Service agencies themselves, however, are not controlled by local churches. Ordination for missionaries working through service agencies is usually provided by their sending churches.

Victory World Missions Outreach. One example of an agency that treats its missionaries like associates and not like employees is Victory World Missions Outreach. The missionaries are free to pursue their call under the authority of their sending and receiving churches, and, most of all, under the Holy Spirit. Victory currently serves about fifty missionaries from forty sending churches. Active in nearly fifty foreign countries, and growing at a rate of seventy percent per year, this missionary force is involved in practically everything from Bible translation to church planting.

For ten percent of the missionaries' monthly income, Victory offers a range of practical and administrative services exceeding that of most mission agencies across the board. Their services include help with financial and educational planning, scheduling, field selection, obtaining visas, and coordinating moving and travel arrangements. They also offer limited representation and promotion, printing and mailing of monthly newsletters, a monthly record of donations and receipts to donors, preparation of tax returns, and help with investments, insurance, wills, and other legal needs. Other services include transportation, housing, counseling while on furlough, medical, dental, and chiropractic care, and regular prayer for specific needs (intercessor on staff).

Victory also provides a number of valuable services to local churches, including missions education for lay people, seminars on missionary preparation in the local church, help in planning a missions strategy, and help in planning annual missions conferences and special missions emphasis programs.

World Outreach Ministries. Founded by Jason R. Peebles of Atlanta, Georgia, World Outreach Ministries is similar to

Victory World Missions Outreach in terms of mission policy, but comparatively limited in the number of services rendered to missionaries. World Outreach is presently serving thirty-eight independent charismatic missionaries in twenty-five countries. These missionaries participate in medical care, orphanages, Bible schools, evangelism, and church planting.[20]

Other examples of service agencies helping independent charismatic missionaries around the globe are In His Service Incorporated in Tulsa, Oklahoma, and Calvary Ministries in Jacksonville, Florida. More of this type of service agency are on the horizon.

Charismatic service agencies add a crucial dimension to the independent charismatic movement. With little bureaucracy and the simplest requirements, they solve the problem of "lone ranger" missionaries launching out with no legal or administrative backing. They free independent missionaries from the often-prohibitive burden of founding their own nonprofit corporations. They fit hand in glove with the free-spirited nature of the charismatic movement, empowering churches and missionaries to fulfill their vision. And they accommodate the widespread charismatic notion that the local church is the only legitimate biblical sending authority for missionaries.

It is possible even for those who do not accept this view of the local church to affirm the sending church/service agency model because of the charismatics' sensitivity to the direction of the Holy Spirit. The real issue of the authority question is not the sending church versus the sending agency, but submission to the sending Spirit—the hallmark of the charismatic movement.

4. *Evangelistic Crusades and Church Planting Crusades.* T. L. Osborn was identified earlier as a pioneer in charismatic missions. A husband and wife team, T. L. and Daisy Osborn have probably preached to more unevangelized people than any couple across history.[21] They hold missionary crusades in various parts of the world, and their current ministry includes training and supporting indigenous ministers abroad.

> Through [the Osborn Foundation in Tulsa, Oklahoma], the Osborns found sponsors for more than 20,000 national preachers as full-time missionaries to their own people. They also provided missionary vehicles, P.A. systems, projectors and screens, films, tapes, and great literature stockpiles in some 50 countries.[22]

Other well-known charismatics involved in crusade evangelism abroad include Oral Roberts' son, Richard, based in Tulsa, Oklahoma, and Reinhard Bonnke, an international evangelist based in Frankfurt, Germany. During the 1980s Bonnke's frequent crusades in Africa attracted crowds of up to 250,000 in one service. Bonnke's team has reported multiple thousands of conversions to Christ, many from the Muslim faith.[23]

Leading missiologists have closely scrutinized this crusade approach to missions. Some researchers, including C. Peter Wagner, have found that ten percent or fewer of those making first-time decisions in crusades become responsible church members.[24] This discrepancy between the number of "decisions" and "disciples" stems from a definition and strategy of evangelism that does not make the grounding of converts in local churches part of the process. Instead, a separate set of activities called "follow-up" is advanced after the tent is folded. The subsequent loss of ninety to ninety-seven percent of the harvest in some crusades is what Wagner calls the "follow-up gap."[25]

In the mid-1970s Edgardo Silvoso, then of the Luis Palau Evangelistic Association, piloted the "Rosario Plan," which helped narrow the follow-up gap in crusade evangelism. First used in Rosario, Argentina, in 1975–76, this approach makes the crusade only one in several components of a twelve-tofifteen-month strategy for planting new churches and getting existing churches in shape for growth. With church growth as the goal, rather than mere professions of faith, the plan has seen as much as fifty-seven to seventy percent of new converts grounded in local churches. This is effective evangelism.[26]

Some Pentecostal-charismatic ministries have also adapted

the crusade model in ways that preserve a greater portion of the harvest. An independent charismatic group in Malaysia, for example, has used the crusade model to gather a nucleus for a new church. Instead of having area local churches "follow up" converts, they simply appoint a trained pastor over them. Larry Stockstill, pastor of Bethany World Prayer Center in Baton Rouge, Louisiana, recently used this method to plant two churches in Russia. Before the crusades were launched, indigenous workers, part of the team effort, were fully prepared to assume pastoral care for the converts. Encouraged by the results in Russia, Stockstill is now planning future church planting crusades for Eastern Europe and other parts of the world.

In the heavily populated Santa Fe area of Argentina, Omar Cabrera's frequent "Vision of the Future" rallies are aided by a team of trained pastors who take responsibility for the new converts. This combination of church growth methodology and crusade evangelism has helped the Vision of the Future movement grow from 30,000 in 1979 to 145,000 by 1988—a growth rate of 2,000 percent in only a decade.[27]

5. AIMS: Networking Charismatic Missions Structures. The Association of International Missions Services (AIMS) is a charismatic organization that does not train or send out missionaries, but links together churches, missions agencies, training institutions, and other unaffiliated Pentecostal-charismatic institutions in cooperative efforts for world evangelization. Some of the charismatic missions agencies described in this book are members of the AIMS network.

AIMS was founded in Dallas, Texas, in 1985 and is currently based in Virginia Beach, Virginia. Their objectives are to develop a consortium of churches and agencies, to assist local churches in missions mobilization, to provide services to mission agencies, to assist training institutions preparing missionaries, to build relationships with other evangelical organizations in the United States and abroad, and to determine overseas needs and develop sister organizations abroad.[28]

Given the lack of an overarching missions structure in the

independent charismatic movement, AIMS plays a key role in nondirective networking of charismatic churches and missions agencies, preserving the autonomy of each group while fostering cooperation and reducing competition and duplication.

This concludes our survey of several major types of church-related and extra-local missions structures emerging from the independent charismatic movement. While we have limited ourselves to a few prominent models, findings show that these models represent typical patterns in independent charismatic missions.

David Shibley's Global Advance, launched in 1990, is a new and distinctive type of charismatic missions organization. Neither a sending nor a service agency, Global Advance is a resourceful, catalytic structure aimed at motivating, equipping, and mobilizing churches, pastors, leaders, young people, and intercessors for world evangelization. Shibley's approach includes conferences, seminars, ministry in churches and on campuses, radio spots, newsletters, and training materials.

Other forms of missions approaches employed by charismatics include "tentmaking" (skilled professionals working and witnessing abroad), tourists in missions (mobilizing of laity), and cross-cultural televangelism (satellite transmission of the Gospel to foreign nations). What is the practical value of such models? What are the goals and results? How could they be redesigned for greater effectiveness? These and many other models of charismatic missions warrant further study. Let us pull together some of what has already been said in this chapter and make a few additional observations.

CHARISMATIC MISSIONS: AN EVALUATION

What is new about charismatic missions? For the most part, the innovations described in this chapter are found in other historic and contemporary church traditions. Even apostolic teams, or rough equivalents to them, functioned for several centuries beyond the early New Testament period.[29]

Even so, there is a distinct freshness about independent charismatic missions. Their innovations are characterized by a spirit of adventure, discovery, and freedom, consistent with the charismatic renewal, and, for that matter, consistent with the nature of the Holy Spirit. In charismatic missions, there is room for gifted leaders to emerge, and ordinary men and women are challenged to attempt extraordinary things for God.

What I have called the pristine dynamics of the Pauline missionary band have largely infused all types of charismatic missions. There is an invigorating sense of having escaped the institutional tyranny that taxes many other traditions, even Pentecostal ones. In 1989, for example, a classical Pentecostal pastor was ousted after preaching in another town without permission from his superiors.[30] Though other issues may have been involved, what would our Pentecostal forebears say about this lapse into patterns of ministry which they once declared too confining?[31] For the most part, charismatic leaders have kept their guard up against this sort of institutional drift.

Charismatic missions are not without shortcomings, however. Some local pastors and even laypersons insist on becoming missions executives, even though they lack the experience, insight, and, the time needed to do the job well. This weakness betrays itself mainly in the area of on-the-field strategy planning, supervision, and evaluation of missionaries in terms of a measurable harvest of saved individuals and growing churches.

It is also true that some church-related and extra-local missions agencies have little or no theory of field selection. Put another way, they lack perspectives on unreached people groups. Many still see the missionary task in geographic terms, out of touch with what the Lausanne movement calls the "people approach to world evangelization."[32]

These problems and others are addressed in chapter 10, where some suggestions are offered toward a more effective charismatic missionary outreach. The next two chapters deal with cultural and theological issues which should be taken seriously by all "Great Commission" Christians and particularly by those in American charismatic churches. In this chapter we have merely sampled a handful of more than one hundred recently formed charismatic missions agencies in the Western world. Add to this some three hundred more based in the Third World.[33] These dynamic, new missions agencies have only begun to tap the vast resources of the tens of thousands of independent charismatic churches in America and around the world. Their flexibility and dependence on the power and leading of the Holy Spirit gives them a strategic missionary edge in today's rapidly changing world.

NOTES

[1]See Peter D. Hocken, "Charismatic Movement," in Stanley M. Burgess and Gary B. McGee, eds. *Dictionary of Pentecostal and Charismatic Movements* (Grand Rapids: Zondervan, 1988), p. 157.

[2]Such mission structures are often called "para-church." But, as argued in chapter 4, the extra-local mission structure is an integral and legitimate part of the New Testament church—its counterpart being the local church structure, the "modality" (a people-oriented, need/nurture-oriented, relation/community-oriented structure by contrast). Paul's Spirit-sent missionary band is the biblical prototype of all subsequent structures for mobilizing individuals in missions beyond the ministry sphere of the local church. See Ralph D. Winter, "The Two Structures of God's Redemptive Mission," in *Perspectives on the World Christian Movement*(Pasadena, Calif.: William Carey Library, 1981), p. 178.

[3]Telephone interviews with Glenda Mayfield, missions secretary, Faith Christian Fellowship International, February 7, 1990, and Robert Buse, director, Faith Christian Fellowship missionary support office, Newark, Delaware, February 15, 1990.

[4]The five stages in Gulf States Missions' training program are as follows: One, the "pastoral care stage" begins in the trainee's home church, under the pastor. It involves personal, spiritual formation, a correspondence course in missions, and practical ministry experience. Stage two, the "candidate stage," is a nine-month intensive training program in Bible, ministry, and missions at Ministers Training Institute, a sister organization to Gulf States Missions. The third stage requires one year of language and culture learning and apprenticeship training under an apostolic minister in El Carmen, Mexico. In stage four, the apprentice becomes an "associate missionary," assisting a senior missionary in some part of the world. At some point, the associate missionary may pioneer a new work or take the helm of an existing one, thus becoming a "senior missionary," entering the fifth and final stage of the training model. Senior missionaries are expected to help train future missionaries on the same model.

⁵Primary sources on Living Water Teaching (LWT) include a packet of promotional literature and unpublished booklets distributed by LWT, and a telephone interview with former LWT missionary, David Henry, February 8, 1990.

⁶C. Peter Wagner, "The Babylonian Captivity of the Christian Mission," paper presented to EFMA-IFMA-AERM Study Conference, Nov. 26–30, 1973, Overland Park, Kansas.

⁷Larry Tomczak, ed. "Unfinished Business, An Interview with Derek Prince," *People of Destiny*, Vol. 4, No. 5, Sept./Oct. 1986, p. 23.

⁸See John Loftness, "Into All the World," *People of Destiny*, Vol. 4, No. 5, Sept./Oct. 1986, p. 18.

⁹Sources on People of Destiny International include: Hocken, "Charismatic Movement," pp. 141f. Larry Tomczak, "The World Mission of Every Christian," *People of Destiny*, Vol. 4, No. 5, Sept./Oct. 1986, p. 15; Tomczak, "Relationship With The Sending Church," in Jim Durkin, et al., *The Church Planter's Handbook* (South Lake Tahoe, Calif.: Christian Equippers International, 1988), p. 105; and a telephone interview with Che Ahn, founder/pastor of Abundant Life Community Church (People of Destiny) in Pasadena, California, February 9, 1990.

¹⁰Important references for the spiritual dynamics of the apostolic team include Edward F. Murphy, "The Missionary Society as an Apostolic Team," *Missiology, An International Review*, Vol. IV, No. 1, Jan. 1976, pp. 114–17; C. Peter Wagner, "Church Growth," in Burgess and McGee, eds., *Dictionary*, p. 194; and Harold R. Cook., "Who Really Sent the First Missionaries?" *Evangelical Missions Quarterly*, Vol. 11, No. 4, Oct. 1975. p. 239.

¹¹See C. M. Irish, "Sharing of Ministries Abroad," in Burgess and McGee, *Dictionary*, p. 783; and Michael Harper, "Renewal For Mission: An Anglican Perspective," *International Review of Mission*, Vol. 75, No. 298, Apr. 1986, p. 131. SOMA (Sharing of Ministries Abroad) is a charismatic organization within the Anglican communion which deploys apostolic teams throughout the world. Also the Gulf States Pastors' Fellowship (independent charismatic), based in the New Orleans area in Louisiana, has also experimented with the apostolic-team approach to church planting.

¹²Wagner, "The Babylonian Captivity," pp. 1f; and Murphy, "The Missionary Society," p. 116.

¹³Primary sources on YWAM include a letter from Loren Cunningham (August 25, 1990) and the following: "Conference on Frontier Missions, Pattaya, Thailand—1989" (a compilation of session notes, case studies, and prayer points); and "Target 2000: All Nations All Peoples" (a 1988 global strategy paper for the last twelve years of the twentieth century). Secondary sources include: Todd Johnson, "YWAM and the Frontiers," *International Journal of Frontier Missions*,

Vol. 1, No. 3, 1984, p. 257; and Dan Wooding, "Loren Cunningham: God's Man Behind YWAM," *Christian Life*, Vol. 48, No. 9, Jan. 1987, p. 38; Grant McClung, ed., *Azusa Street and Beyond*(South Plainfield: N.J., Bridge, 1986), pp. 145–46.

[14]Larry Pate, *From Every People* (Monrovia, Calif.: MARC, 1989), p. 51.

[15]Wooding quoting Cunningham in "Loren Cunningham," p. 38.

[16]Pate, *From Every People*, p. 105.

[17]Sources on Globe Missionary Evangelism include their promotional literature and two telephone interviews with Josh Peters, Globe's assistant missions director, August 9, 1988, and February 12, 1990. See also Michele Buckingham, "Retaining the Excitement That Motivates Missions," *Ministries*, Vol. 4, No. 3, Summer 1986, p. 44.

[18]Sources on World Indigenous Missions include their current brochures, a letter from Michael J. Costello, administrator (December 18, 1989), and a telephone interview with Chuck Hall, one of their missionaries studying at Fuller Theological Seminary, School of World Mission, Pasadena, Calif., February 7, 1990.

[19]The quotation and the information that follows are taken from some of the promotional literature of Victory World Missions Outreach, supplemented by a telephone interview with founding director, Gary Rechtfertig, February 16, 1990.

[20]World Outreach Ministries brochure. Telephone interview with Steve Schultz, missions director, February 13, 1990.

[21]Willard Mason and James Kerby, "Oklahoma: Charismatic Crossroads of America," *Christian Life*, Vol. 47, No. 4, Aug. 1985, p. 20.

[22]Ibid., p. 21.

[23]Vinson Synan, "Bonnke, Reinhard Willi Gottfried," in Burgess and McGee, eds., *Dictionary*, p. 93.

[24]Wagner, C. Peter, *Strategies for Church Growth* (Ventura, Calif.: Regal Books, 1987), p. 138; See also Edward R. Dayton and David A. Fraser, *Planning Strategies for World Evangelization* (Grand Rapids: Eerdmans, 1980), p. 373.

[25]Wagner, *Strategies*, p. 139.

[26]Ibid., pp. 149–50; See also Dayton and Fraser, *Planning Strategies*, pp. 373–74 (Rosario Plan and results).

[27]C. Peter Wagner, *The Third Wave of the Holy Spirit* (Ann Arbor, Mich.: Vine Books/Servant Publications, 1988), pp. 97–99; and Wagner, *Spiritual Power and Church Growth* (Altamonte Springs, Fla.: Strang Communications), p. 28.

[28]See Gary B. McGee, "Association of International Missions Services (AIMS)," in Burgess and McGee, eds., *Dictionary*, p. 30. My list is part quotation and part paraphrase of McGee's.

[29]Murphy, "The Missionary Society," p. 115.

[30]Stephen Strang, ed., "Assemblies Pastor Ousted from Pulpit," *Charisma & Christian Life*, Vol. 15, No. 6, Jan. 1990, p. 20.

[31]See Donald W. Dayton, "The Holiness and Pentecostal Churches: Emerging from Cultural Isolation," *The Christian Century*, Vol. 96, No. 26, Aug. 1979, p. 786. On page 787 he writes, "Holiness and Pentecostal folk are busily engaged in creating all those agencies and patterns of church life that their maverick forebears found too confining."

[32]See Dayton and Fraser, *Planning Strategies*, pp. 109ff.

[33]See David B. Barrett, "Statistics, Global," in Burgess and McGee, eds., *Dictionary*, p. 830.

Charisma and Culture: Anthropological Insights for Charismatic Missions

———+———

Chapter 8

The baptism in the Holy Spirit, or the baptism of the American dream? The Gospel of the kingdom, or the gospel of King's kids? The Bread of Life, or the loaves and fishes? These questions on the norms of gospel and society are difficult ones for American Christians. This is especially true for those in the independent charismatic movement, as we shall see.

Thus far we have examined the origins, aspects, and missionary methods of independent charismatic ministries based in the United States. The next chapter will bring the biblical theology of missions to bear upon charismatic theology, and the last chapter will address key missions strategy issues for independent charismatics. This chapter attempts to apply insights from missionary anthropology to the independent charismatic movement, issues that were first introduced in chapter 3.

In some ways charismatic churches have challenged American culture, but in other ways the movement has capitulated. Many have argued that charismatics make the best missionaries even though they often carry excess cultural baggage that impedes missionary effectiveness. For the sake of the three billion unevangelized people in today's world, some hard questions need to be asked.

CHARISMATICS' CAPITULATION
TO AMERICAN CULTURE

How much of charismatic Christianity is "gospel," and how much of it is merely a reflection of our late twentieth-century American world? In other words, to what extent have we accepted the cultural norms of our society, and how does this limit or impede our effectiveness in world evangelization?[1]

Pentecostalism's Upward Mobility.   We must begin our quest for answers with a reflection on our roots. Early Pentecostalism, we have noted, began as a counter-culture movement on the "poor side of town." Early Pentecostals seemed out of step with the times. Their prophetic gospel challenged the rich and worldly but consoled and lifted the poor. As religious scholar Grant Wacker observes, "the movement survived, not in spite of the fact that it was out of step with the times, but precisely because it was."[2]

During the 1950s, however, "tongues moved uptown." Postwar prosperity lifted the movement to new material heights. As we saw previously, leading preachers of the healing movement left the sawdust trail for carpeted Hilton ballrooms, attracting more sophisticated audiences. By the 1960s, the Pentecostal-charismatic movement had become a middle-class phenomenon. Did we grow up? Wacker does not think so: "In crucial respects, the Pentecostal movement is less mature today than it was in the early years."[3]

Implications for World Missions.   In some ways, accommodation to middle-class America drastically alters our understanding of the Gospel. Early Pentecostals felt a special calling to avoid materialism, living their lives in simplicity and self-denial. But thousands of charismatics today have come to see salvation primarily in terms of its byproducts, physical health and worldly success, rather than its claims on our life. This limits the impact of the Gospel and impedes world evangelization in at least four ways.

1. Loaves and Fishes Conversions.   First, this "gospel" invites people to follow Christ for the "loaves and fishes." I remember, for example, my first evangelistic sermon in Ghana, West Africa. At first there was no response. Then, in an apparent effort to save face (mine), my interpreter added the health and wealth appeal. Suddenly about fifty villagers streamed to the altar to pray the sinner's prayer. But when we invited them to the river for baptism, they all scattered in different directions. Only six teenagers remained and quietly followed us to the river for baptism.

Admittedly, the motive for conversion is not as determinative as postbaptismal teaching and care. But my first African converts were obviously not following Christ—they were after "loaves and fishes," physical health and worldly success. This same act is played out in large scale around the world as charismatic evangelists multiply "decisions" for Christ based on what Paul Yonggi Cho calls a "sugar-coated gospel."[4]

2. The Gospel of the "Haves" to the "Have-nots." The baptized materialism of the American church tends to distance us from the plight of the masses of the Third World and urban poor, a major mission field of today. In Haiti, for example, a needy national pastor once asked a charismatic faith teacher for money. "You can get yours like I get mine," said the faith teacher. "Use your faith."

This idea of faith is everything *but* good news to the poor. It overlooks the political and sociological forces that cause poverty. This kind of response plunges the poor into deeper discouragement by blaming their poverty on their own so-called lack of faith. As we know, faith is not the real issue.

3. The Jet-set Versus the Ox Cart. A materialistic view of salvation also denies Christ's call to a simple lifestyle of cross-bearing servanthood, which is essential for the spread of the Gospel to the unreached. We too easily justify our lavish models of ministry and missions. "Surely," we say, "if Paul or Jesus were here today, they would use the world's best innovations and technologies." Maybe. However, Jesus and Paul did not even use Roman chariots.

Let me illustrate. As a young American missionary in Ghana, I used to drive my imported Ford Granada through the small town where I lived. Air-conditioner on, power-windows up, the sounds and smells of humble humanity were neatly blocked out. But one day my "chariot" was stolen. Suddenly I found myself walking the village streets, riding public transport, and breathing dust and fumes like most Ghanaian citizens. Gradually I began to feel the heartbeat of the people I was trying to reach. Then they discovered that I too had a heart. As a result, I became a better missionary.

For most of the world's unreached peoples, the "ox cart" model of ministry is more effective than the "jet-set" approach. But a faith that makes the benefits of the Cross the center of the Gospel can hardly produce the kind of self-effacing servants needed to touch the hearts of the masses with the love of Christ today.

4. The Neutralizing Effect of Trends and Fads. America's obsession with trends and fads has also impacted our charismatic version of Christianity, as witnesses this word by J. I. Packer:

> Culturally, the charismatic movement appears as a child of our time in its antitraditionalism, its anti-intellectualism, its romantic emotionalism, its desire for thrills and emotional highs, its narcissistic preoccupation with physical health and ease of mind, its preferences for folk-type music with poetically uncouth lyrics, and its cultivated informality. In all these respects, the renewal reflects the late twentieth-century Western world back at itself.[5]

While it is sometimes useful and usually inevitable that Christians incorporate a certain amount of contemporary cultural form into their experience (or else, as Paul said in 1 Corinthians 5:10, we "would have to leave this world"), we need to be aware how much we really are children of our time.

As journalist Jamie Buckingham writes, "Both American culture and American Christianity . . . operate on fad."[6] New "revelations" vie for attention, pulling us this way and that. One year, everyone has a demon. The next year, everyone wants to be rich. Then we are going to get raptured tomorrow. So there is no point trying to change the world today.

Perhaps some of these emphases find limited expression in Scripture and have some practical value. But none of them are central to the Gospel. To achieve balance, these teachings must be subjected to the broader theological framework of Scripture and historical Christian orthodoxy. They must also be brought into conformity with God's redemptive concern for perishing humanity. For, as Howard Foltz writes, "Trends and fads within the renewal movement that are not strategically rooted in the completion of God's mission tend to weaken its involvement in world evangelization."[7]

A Microcosm of the American Church. The American church's capitulation to its surrounding culture is not just a Pentecostal-charismatic phenomenon. Richard J. Foster, author of *Money, Sex, and Power*, had this to say about the PTL scandal of 1987:

> . . .what happened to Jim and Tammy Bakker is only a microcosm of a condition which permeates the church in the United States today. PTL is not an isolated incident, but a sign of the sickness of the church. On the whole, the American church has embraced wholeheartedly the values of our society.[8]

These issues apply to all American Christians. Individually and corporately, the church in this country needs to ask how our response to Christ has been conditioned by our unconscious acceptance of cultural norms and how this limits the impact of our message to the unchurched both here and abroad.

How has the charismatic movement challenged our culture, and how has this influenced world missions in positive ways?[9] There are at least four significant ways in which charismatic churches are exerting a positive influence on Western culture.

THE CHARISMATIC CHALLENGE
TO CULTURE AND ITS
IMPACT ON MISSIONS

1. A Challenge to Secularism. First of all, the charismatic movement, and especially the nondenominational segment of the movement, has effectively challenged the Western gods of secular science and antisupernaturalism.[10] Some of the outcries against the charismatic faith movement are but echoes of our own scientific age.[11] Healing by prayer, victory over demons, and guidance by spiritual gifts have presented a refreshing alternative to a rationalistic form of faith that sees miracles as a thing of the past.

This resurgence of interest in the supernatural represents a positive contribution to the cause of world evangelization. The reason for this is that for decades Western missionaries exported to the Third World a Gospel that failed to address the supernatural realm. Medical science replaced traditional, non-Christian forms of exorcism and healing. The result was that Christianity became a secularizing force in the Third World.[12]

This approach to missions has been challenged by the Pentecostal-charismatic movement. Missionary theologian Arthur F. Glasser of Fuller Theological Seminary writes:

> . . .Pentecostals were willing to tackle the "dark side of the soul" and challenge the growing phenomenon of occultism, Satan worship, and demon possession. Whereas IFMA people and other non-charismatic evangelicals (particularly the Baptists!) had found it relatively easy to expose the extravagance of the occasional charlatan, they were silenced in the presence of the Pentecostal's serious confrontation of the hard realities of the spirit world. Here was a spirituality which could not be ignored.[13]

Today, missionaries from various traditions, even non-charismatic ones, expect God to confirm his Word through visible demonstrations of his power over demons and disease. As we have previously noted, some researchers have found that eighty percent of current conversions from paganism to Christianity occur as a result of the ministry of signs and wonders.[14]

2. *A Challenge to Cerebral Christianity.* Related to the challenge to secularism is the charismatic movement's chal-

lenge to dry, intellectualized forms of faith, worship, and spirituality. "The 'non-charismatic' church is very often a cerebralized church that appeals only to a very small part of the human personality," says European charismatic leader and scholar Arnold Bittlinger.[15] In contrast to much of traditional evangelicalism, charismatic worship typically combines oral theology, spontaneous liturgy, contemporary music, prophecy, and tongues-speaking, creating a "cathedral of sounds," celebrating the God of the "here and now."[16] This impacts cross-cultural missions in positive ways.

For example, many religions of the Third World are simply expressions of the constant human quest for well-being and spiritual security. Belief systems are designed to make some sense out of a world full of the unpredictable and the unexplainable. Through endless rituals and ceremonies, devotees try to appease angry and capricious gods. In such settings, charismatic forms of faith have made a phenomenal impact around the world. Lively worship styles and need-oriented preaching appeal to masses who are unattracted to historic, institutionalized Christianity.[17] Bittlinger writes,

> Charismatic experiences are frequently clothed in [non-rational] phenomena [such as pictures, acts, music, and movement] and thus speak directly to the human heart. Not surprisingly, therefore, charismatic services are well-attended and especially in places where people are not particularly interested in "normal" acts of worship. . . . Charismatic experiences are healing experiences for the whole person.[18]

Charismatic missionaries naturally awaken hope in a God who heals diseases; silences screaming demons; showers crops with rain; and speaks to his children in dreams, visions, and prophecy. A gospel that addresses the spiritual, emotional, physical, and material needs of humans is indeed good news to the world. Ralph Winter's statement on this is significant:

Already it is obvious that the world church is rapidly taking on the cultural characteristics of the so-called pentecostal-charismatic tradition. This shift is being resisted, but mainly by nongrowing groups. Our modern world is now irretrievably more of an emotion-accepting world. It is no longer only at football games that the full range of human emotions can be expressed.[19]

3. A Challenge to Western Individualism. Charismatics have also challenged America's "rugged individualism," a byproduct of the nineteenth-century frontier movement and late-twentieth-century urbanization. Perhaps the violent reactions in the 1970s against the discipleship movement are not unrelated to the lone-ranger mentality of the West. But despite the independence of nondenominational charismatic churches, local fellowships exhibit close personal relationships and loyal interdependence between their members. The Greek New Testament calls this *koinonia*. Body ministry and team leadership make charismatic Christianity a highly corporate affair.

This has positive implications for missions in at least three ways. First, most Third World peoples are more relationship-oriented than Westerners. Second, charismatic churches are noted for producing missionaries who have the local church at heart and who are committed to planting and strengthening local churches on the field. Third, this communal spirit fosters an effective team approach to pioneer ministry and church planting.

For example, Larry Tomczak, the leader of the People of Destiny movement, sees team ministry as a key to a new wave of kingdom expansion. Tomczak writes, "Apostolic ministry is not a flash of brilliant individualism, but it is a glorious teamwork."[20] In the People of Destiny's apostolic team approach to church planting, leaders are trained in local churches, organized in teams where each member's gifts complement the others, and sent out to plant new churches. During the 1980s People of Destiny planted twenty-one new churches using the team approach.

Youth With A Mission is another Pentecostal-charismatic

organization demonstrating a community-based, team-oriented approach to ministry and missions. "All in all it can be said that the [charismatic movement] has presented a biblically sound challenge to the current idol of Western individualism," writes South African theologian Henry Lederle.[21]

4. Charismatics Meet the Social Challenge. Charismatics may still lack much of a theology of social ministry, but as in all new movements, including early Christianity, theology follows practice. On the structural level, charismatics have been active and effective in moral protests, mercy ministries, and social transformation.

One example of such activity is the widespread independent charismatic support for Operation Rescue, a nationwide movement against legalized abortion. Many pastors and church members have been jailed for their active protests at medical clinics that perform abortions.

In the area of social service, some of the churches associated with Earl Paulk and the "kingdom-now" movement are actively involved in ministry to the underprivileged in the inner-city.[22] And in 1978 the Christian Broadcasting Network (CBN), a Virginia-based charismatic organization led by Pat Robertson, formed "Operation Blessing." This arm of CBN became one of America's largest private organizations helping the poor. Also, in 1985 CBN began "Operation Heads Up," a nationwide program teaching illiterate persons how to read.[23]

In South Africa, dozens of Rhema churches, associated with Kenneth Hagin and the faith movement, have been among the most compassionate and generous Christians in that country, according to South African pastor Allan Anderson.

> Far from abandoning their responsibilities towards the poor, these Christians see it as their God-given duty to do what they can to alleviate poverty—and not just through the proclamation of "prosperity," but in practical giving![24]

In addition to this, a 1987 study by two professors from the University of Calgary, Alberta, shows that South African independent charismatics have played a leading role in the move to abolish apartheid. In their article in *The Christian Century*, researchers Irving Hexham and Karla Poewe-Hexham say the following:

> Since 1979, hundreds of new, independent charismatic churches have formed throughout South Africa. They bridge racial barriers as no other groups do. For years mainline churches like the Anglicans, Lutherans and Roman Catholics have talked about reconciliation and multiracialism, but their weekly services have achieved only tokenism. The new charismatics are different.[25]

The article also describes a 1987 multiracial conference, "GO-FEST," which was organized by the charismatic-oriented Youth With A Mission. During the week-long conference, five thousand young South Africans of all races met, sang, danced, and ate together, even sharing living quarters.

According to the Hexham article, independent charismatic churches in South Africa are twenty-to-sixty percent black, and leadership is shared with blacks. For example, a 12,000 member Rhema church in Randbury is twenty-five percent black. A 250-member Vineyard Fellowship which meets alternately in Johannesburg and Soweto is jointly led by a black and a white pastor.

Considering indications that nearly thirty-five percent of all South Africans participate in some way in the charismatic movement, these great, nonviolent strides toward racial equality by independent charismatics are more than talk and tokenism. As the Hexham report says,

> Though political equality and complete justice for blacks is still a long way off, it is no longer out of sight. Internal cultural change is providing hope. In the forefront are the charismatics, who are offering blacks and whites alike a new vision of the future. This hopeful vision of a land where all South Africans live together under the Lordship of Christ is the charismatics' greatest contribution to the nation's gloom and increasing political violence.[26]

These are not isolated examples of a few charismatic philanthropists and social activists. Rather, this is somewhat typical of many charismatic churches and groups responding to social needs and challenges in the United States and abroad. This obedience to biblical injunctions to Christian social responsibility is an integral part of fulfilling the biblical missionary mandate.

CHARISMA, CULTURE, AND MISSIONS

We have considered some of the strengths and weaknesses of the charismatic movement in general. What has been said also applies to the independent charismatic movement. Charismatics, we have seen, are more culture-embracing than their Pentecostal forebears. This is not wrong in itself, but having embraced a form of sanctified materialism and self-fulfillment, we have gone too far. The "five thousand" have been fed and overfed. Perceptive leaders in the movement are seeing that it is time to break the Bread of Life for the unreached peoples of the world. But to maximize our missionary effectiveness, we need to face the kinds of issues raised here and in the next chapter.

On the positive side, we have shown how charismatics have challenged certain aspects of Western culture and traditional Christianity. They have introduced forms of faith and worship that speak to the needs of human hearts around the world. All this enhances their potential to "be a blessing" to the peoples of the earth.

NOTES

[1]See Eugene L. Stockwell, "Editorial" (on the Charismatic Movement and Christian Mission), *International Review of Mission*, Vol. 75, No. 298, Apr. 1986, p. 113. On p. 116 Stockwell raises the question ". . .regarding the ways in which contemporary Chris-

tianity has accepted almost unconsciously many of the cultural norms of society, western or eastern, that limit or even impede the full flowering of the gospel in all its meaning and impact in our contemporary world. All of us, charismatics or not, must wrestle with the danger, seeking to understand how our culture affects our faith and how our response to the Spirit may be adversely affected by our easy acceptance of cultural norms." This insightful statement by Stockwell sets the tone for the issues raised in this chapter.

[2]Grant Wacker, "America's Pentecostals: Who They Are," *Christianity Today*, Vol. 31, No. 15, Oct. 16, 1987, p. 21.

[3]Ibid., p. 21.

[4]Stephen Strang, "Cho's Problem With Prosperity," *Charisma & Christian Life*, Vol. 13, No. 8, Mar. 1988, p. 71. Addressing "Spirit-filled" Christians in the United States, Cho says, "You have stressed the blessings of the kingdom so much that you are proclaiming a sugar-coated gospel. People hear that in the kingdom they get free of charge salvation, baptism in the Spirit, spiritual gifts, divine healing, blessings. They have not heard enough that they must repent and keep the law of God if they are to enjoy the blessings of the kingdom."

[5]J. I. Packer, "Piety on Fire," *Christianity Today*, Vol. 33, No. 8, May 12, 1989, p. 20.

[6]Jamie Buckingham, "Charismatic Fads," *Ministries Today*, Vol. 7, No. 1, Jan./Feb., 1989, p. 14.

[7]Howard Foltz, "Moving Toward a Charismatic Theology of Missions," *Probing Pentecostalism* (The Society for Pentecostal Studies, 17th Annual Meeting, Nov. 12–14, 1987, CBN University, Virginia Beach, Virginia), p. 78.

[8]Richard J. Foster, "The PTL Scandal," *Charisma & Christian Life*, Vol. 13, No. 8, Mar. 1988, p. 40.

[9]See Henry I. Lederle, "The Charismatic Movement—The Ambiguous Challenge," *Missionalia*, Vol. 14, No. 2, Aug. 1986, p. 61. This article provides rich background and inspiration for my discussion on the charismatic movement's challenge to culture.

[10]Lederle, "The Charismatic Movement." This South African theologian writes, "The [charismatic renewal movement] has opened up the whole realm of the so-called 'supernatural' with fresh enthusiasm. . . . This presents a serious challenge to the accepted ways of thinking in modernity and the scientific mind-set of Western civilisation" (p. 74).

[11]Bruce Barron, *The Health and Wealth Gospel* (Downers Grove, Ill.: InterVarsity Press, 1987). On page 81 Barron writes, "Whether we find [the faith teachers'] view extreme or not, we must give them credit for rediscovering a truth that the early church welcomed. Perhaps we are more children of our own scientific age than we care to admit."

[12]Paul G. Hiebert, "The Flaw of the Excluded Middle," *Missiol-*

ogy: An International Review, Vol. X, No. 1, Jan. 1982, p. 35. On p. 46 he says, "So long as the missionary comes with a two-tier worldview with God confined to the supernatural, and the natural world operating for all practical purposes according to autonomous scientific laws, Christianity will continue to be a secularizing force in the world. Only as God is brought back into the middle of our scientific understanding of nature will we stem the tide of Western secularism."

[13]Arthur F. Glasser and Donald A. McGavran, *Contemporary Theologies of Mission*(Grand Rapids: Baker, 1983), pp. 119–20.

[14]See Larry Pate, *From Every People* (Monrovia, Calif.: MARC, 1989), p. 127; David Shibley, *A Force in the Earth* (Altamonte Springs, Fla.: Creation House, 1989), p. 36; and C. Peter Wagner, *Spiritual Power and Church Growth* (Altamonte Springs, Fla.: Strang Communications, 1986), p. 12.

[15]Arnold Bittlinger, "The Significance of Charismatic Experiences for the Mission of the Church," *International Review of Mission*, Vol. 75, No. 298, Apr. 1986, p. 120.

[16]See Walter J. Hollenweger, "Charismatic Renewal in the Third World: Implications for Mission," *Occasional Bulletin of Missionary Research*, Vol. 4, No. 2, Apr. 1980, p. 70.

[17]See Foltz, "Moving Toward a Charismatic Theology," p. 77; and Stockwell, "Editorial," p. 116.

[18]Bittlinger, "The Significance," p. 121. See also Allan Anderson, "The Prosperity Message in the Eschatology of Some New Charismatic Churches," *Missionalia*, Vol. 15, No. 2, Aug. 1987, pp. 81–82.

[19]Ralph D. Winter, "Mission in the 1990s," *International Bulletin of Missionary Research*, Vol. 14, No. 3, July 1990, p. 100.

[20]Larry Tomczak, "Relationship With the Sending Church," in Jim Durkin, et al., *The Church Planters Handbook* (South Lake Tahoe, Calif.: Christian Equippers International, 1988), p. 108. See also Tomczak, "The World Mission of Every Christian," *People of Destiny*, Vol. 4, No. 5, Sept./Oct. 1986, p. 17.

[21]Lederle, "The Charismatic Movement," p. 73.

[22]See Stephen Strang, ed., "Rock Church Ignites National Food Drive," *Charisma & Christian Life*, Vol. 14, No. 7, Feb. 1989, p. 31.

[23]Wayne E. Warner, "Robertson, Marion Gordon ('Pat')," in Stanley M. Burgess and Gary B. McGee, eds., *Dictionary of Pentecostal and Charismatic Movements* (Grand Rapids: Zondervan, 1988), p. 762.

[24]Anderson, "The Prosperity Message," p. 79.

[25]Irving Hexham and Karla Poewe-Hexham, "Charismatics and Change in South Africa," *The Christian Century*, Aug. 17–24, 1988, p. 738.

[26]Ibid., p. 740. On indications that nearly thirty-five percent of South Africans are involved in the charismatic movement, see p. 738.

A Second Blessing of a Different Sort: Moving Charismatics Toward A Biblical Theology of Missions

———————+———————

Chapter 9

Pentecostal-charismatics sometimes refer to the baptism of the Holy Spirit as the "second blessing." The author of Genesis spoke of a second blessing of a different sort: The first blessing was for Abraham: ". . .I will bless you; I will make your name great. . ." (Gen. 12:2). The second blessing was for all the peoples of the world: ". . .and all peoples on earth will be blessed through you" (v.3). As children of Abraham and heirs of the so-called Full Gospel, many American charismatics are yet to come to terms with the missiological implications of this promised blessing to the nations. As Oswald J. Smith wrote, "We talk about the second blessing. They haven't had the first blessing yet."[1]

Howard Foltz summarizes the problem this way: ". . .the charismatic movement suffers from an inadequate theology of mission."[2] This was identified in chapter 5 as one of the hindrances to missions mobilization by independent charismatics, a need which sets the agenda for what follows—a humble attempt to help charismatics get in closer touch with evangelical missions theology.

This chapter is neither an overview of evangelical missions theology nor a thorough exposition of the theology of the independent charismatic movement. Though I differ with charismatic teaching at several points, my purpose is not to criticize. Rather, this chapter is a dialogue of sorts, showing how evangelical missions theology can enrich and impact major charismatic teachings. Conversely, it stresses that certain distinctives of charismatic theology can likewise enrich current evangelical missions theology.

CHARISMATIC THEOLOGY

Emerging from the charismatic renewal, independent charismatic churches generally hold to basic doctrines of evangelicalism on most points. Supporting this claim is a statement by J. I. Packer, a distinguished critic of the charismatic renewal:

> Doctrinally, the renewal is in the mainstream of historic evangelical orthodoxy on the Trinity, the Incarnation, the objectivity of Christ's atonement and the historicity of his resurrection, the need of regeneration by the Holy Spirit, personal fellowship with the Father and the Son as central to the life of faith, and the divine truth of the Bible.[3]

However, independent charismatics are noted (if not notorious) for certain theological distinctives which set them apart from evangelicals and, in some cases, even Pentecostals. Charismatic teachings on faith, wealth, ongoing revelation, and positive thinking and confession, for example, are not typically Pentecostal or evangelical. Charismatics stress tongues-speaking and spiritual gifts in public worship more than Pentecostals do. And for charismatics, the postconversion Spirit-baptism is to be received, not by "long tarrying" as in early Pentecostalism, but simply by faith.[4]

The independent charismatic movement, having begun in the 1970s, is too young and diverse to have a systematic theology as such. A giant step in this direction is *Renewal Theology*, a three-volume work by J. Rodman Williams, theology professor at Regent University (formerly CBNU) in Virginia, and published by Academie Books of Zondervan Publishing House. This will become a major resource for independent charismatics. Even so, *Renewal Theology* does not necessarily represent the theology of the independent charismatic movement as a whole, given the many divergent streams of this movement.[5]

CHARISMATIC STREAMS AND THEMES

Each of the five major streams within the independent charismatic movement, described below, has its own set of emphases. However, there is much overlap between these groupings and their teachings. They are not mutually exclusive, and the list is far from exhaustive. It is fairly representative, however, and helps us to see what is possibly the beginnings of a charismatic theological system.

1. The Faith Movement. A swelling stream in the independent charismatic movement, the faith movement espouses a unique theology based largely on the teachings of Kenneth E. Hagin, Sr., and E. W. Kenyon. The basic tenets of faith teaching are financial prosperity; divine healing; positive thinking and confession; success in life; revelation knowledge; and the believer's authority over Satan, demons, and negative circumstances through identification with Christ.

Kenneth E. Hagin, Kenneth and Gloria Copeland, Jerry Savelle, Fred Price, Robert Tilton, and Charles Capps are among the leading teachers of the faith movement. Thousands of charismatic churches and ministers espouse faith teachings, and hundreds of them relate together in loose associations or networks, such as the International Convention of Faith Churches and Ministries, and the Association of Faith Churches and Ministries, both of which are based in Tulsa, Oklahoma.

Faith teachings are so widely accepted by charismatics that, according to Dan McConnell's *A Different Gospel*, ". . .in the minds of many [the faith movement] is no longer just a *part* of the charismatic movement: it *is* the charismatic movement."[6]

2. Kingdom-Now. Another significant stream in the independent charismatic movement emphasizes a theology known as "kingdom-now." Earl Paulk, pastor of the ten-thousand-member Chapel Hill Harvester Church in Atlanta, Georgia, and Tommy Reid, pastor of Full Gospel Tabernacle of Orchard Park, New York, are among the leading kingdom-now teachers.

Kingdom-now theology urges Christian involvement in

social reform. As the "salt of the earth," believers are to demonstrate the presence of the kingdom of God by infiltrating societal structures and bringing about productive change in the secular order. Other themes of the kingdom message include restorationism (restoring New Testament church principles), divine healing, deliverance from demons, unity of the church, spiritual authority (or, covering), and the "fivefold ministry" of apostle, prophet, evangelist, pastor, and teacher (Eph. 4:11).[7]

3. *Covenant Churches.* The discipleship-shepherding era which began in the 1970s has perhaps ended. But the basic principles of the movement continue to influence many independent charismatic churches.[8] For example, in 1987 Charles Simpson, one of the key leaders in the discipleship movement, founded the Fellowship of Covenant Ministers and Churches based in Mobile, Alabama. This group had 250 churches by 1988.[9]

Maranatha Campus Ministries and its parent organization, Maranatha Christian Churches, began in 1972 under the ministry of Bob Weiner. Until 1990, Maranatha functioned under a form of shepherding-type authority, although they have probably had more in common with the faith movement.[10] Maranatha modified its structure in January 1990, allowing the individual churches across the nation and around the world to function autonomously.

Discipleship teaching emphasizes the need for believers to submit to spiritual leaders who represent God's authority in the body of Christ. There have been abuses in this area. But at the heart of discipleship teaching are healthy emphases on self-denial, radical obedience to Christ, and growth to maturity in the context of covenant relationships with other believers.

4. *Restorationist Charismatics.* Restorationist currents are strong in various groupings of independent charismatic churches and ministers. These churches emphasize the end-time restoration of God's New Testament patterns of church life. They stress the nine spiritual gifts of 1 Corinthians 12 and, in particular, the "fivefold ministry" gifts of Ephesians 4:11 as

God's true order for church government. God is now restoring the apostolic and prophetic dimensions of churchly authority, according to this view.

With some links to the restorationist (house church) movement in Britain, People of Destiny International (PDI), led by Larry Tomczak, is one of several groups emphasizing restorationist principles. As we saw earlier, their apostolic team exercises an extra-local authority in church planting and church government. PDI leaders painstakingly stress the spiritual, relational character of their authority.

Similar restorationist emphases and patterns of church government are seen in churches associated with Jim Jackson of the National Leadership Conference based in Montreat, North Carolina. Lastly, the New Covenant Commission (formerly based in Tulsa, Oklahoma, but now dissolved) functioned in restorationist principles.[11]

5. *The Signs and Wonders Movement.* Virtually all segments of the independent charismatic movement stress the ministry of signs and wonders. But the Association of Vineyard Churches, led by John Wimber of Anaheim, California, has become a flagship of sorts for the emphasis on signs and wonders, power evangelism, and power healing. There are some three hundred Vineyard churches representing a total of more than five thousand members. Influenced in part by the Fuller Theological Seminary School of World Mission in Pasadena, California, Wimber grounds his theology of signs and wonders not only in the ministry of the Holy Spirit but in the New Testament teaching on the kingdom of God.[12]

Both the shape and size of the Vineyard movement is changing, however, since their 1990 "adoption" of the so-called "Kansas City Prophets," a controversial charismatic group led by Paul Cain, Jack Deere, and others. This prophetically-oriented group is based in Kansas City Fellowship, a church in Kansas City, Missouri.

These groups constitute the major centers of influence shaping the thought and theology of the independent charismatic movement. The movement knows many other streams and themes, but those described here typify its central personalities and teachings. From these we can draw up a list of headings delineating some of the major theological emphases of the independent charismatic movement:

The baptism of the Holy Spirit (overarching and basically inherited from classical Pentecostalism)

The power and gifts of the Spirit for ministry (signs and wonders and prophetic ministry)

Restoration of New Testament church principles (the five-fold ministry and spiritual gifts)

Spiritual warfare and power over Satan and demons

Divine healing by prayer and the laying on of hands

Faith and positive confession for health, success, and prosperity

Authority over Satan by identification with Christ (dominion and kingdom-now theologies)

Discipleship/shepherding (covenant relationships)

Many critics have questioned the orthodoxy of these teachings. Here we are content to show how themes from the biblical theology of missions can and should impact charismatic teachings. Such an exchange would bring further balance to the independent charismatic movement and generate a more effective missionary outreach on the part of its churches.

MISSION THEOLOGY IMPACTS CHARISMATIC TEACHINGS

Biblical theology of missions is a broad discipline which includes several major themes such as the biblical basis of missions in both testaments, the kingdom of God, the fate of the lost, the missionary nature of the church, Christian social responsibility, the Great Commission mandate, non-Christian religions, and much more. The following shows how major charismatic teachings serve as natural entry points for incorporating certain themes from the biblical theology of missions into charismatic theology.

1. *The Holy Spirit and Missions.* The Pentecostal-charismatic emphasis on the Holy Spirit can be seen as a first example. Roland Allen, a pioneer missiologist in the early twentieth century, saw the central nature and ministry of the Spirit in terms of the missionary outreach of the church. Most charismatic teachers of our day, however, ignore this aspect of the Spirit's ministry, even though they intuitively know that their charismatic experiences should affect world outreach.[13] Consequently, in the minds of many charismatics, the receiving of the Spirit is not firmly and theologically grounded in the spiritual sending of the church into all the world. What follows is a sample of Roland Allen's arguments in his *Missionary Principles*. It shows how missions theology can broaden our understanding of the nature and ministry of the Holy Spirit.[14]

When Jesus said, "Receive the Holy Spirit," it was in the context of a divine sending: "As the Father has sent me, I am sending you" (John 20:21). Likewise, the promise of the Spirit in Acts 1:8 was linked to the mandate of worldwide witness.

The gift of tongues at Pentecost, understood by visiting pilgrims from all over the then-known world, symbolically foreshadowed the cross-cultural communication of the Gospel to all peoples of the earth. And the missionary thrust launched from Antioch in Acts 13 was first and foremost a divine sending by the Holy Spirit. "So, being sent out by the Holy Spirit, they went. . ." (Acts 13:4, RSV).

In Roland Allen's thought, the fact that the first apostles and the New Testament epistles hardly ever mentioned the Great Commission shows that the primary impulse for missions in the early church was not a legalistic adherence to Christ's command, but the missionary heartbeat of the Spirit of Pentecost. He writes:

> The moment that we recognize the Spirit in us as a Spirit of missions, we know that we are not partakers of Christ for ourselves alone, we know that the Church which does not conquer the world dies. To luxuriate in the rich pastures. . . becomes an absurdity, a denial of the life, a denial of the grace given to us.[15]

The Holy Spirit not only sanctifies, edifies, and empowers, he also sends and commissions the church into worldwide ministry. A.B. Simpson, founder of the Christian and Missionary Alliance, once said, "the best way to be filled with the Spirit is to be true to the great thrust for which he was given—the evangelization of the world."[16] A rediscovery of this missionary ministry of the Spirit is essential if the independent charismatic church movement is to make its greatest possible contribution to the cause of world evangelization.

2. Signs and Wonders. Consider the charismatic teaching on signs and wonders and the power of the Spirit for supernatural ministry. The independent charismatic movement teaches and claims the power promises of the New Testament, but rarely does it pay heed to the context of these promises— the Great Commission. The New Testament promises of spiritual power commonly claimed by charismatics are directly linked to the worldwide mission of the church. Consider these examples from the Gospels and Acts (emphasis mine):

> *All authority* in heaven and on earth has been given to me. Therefore go and make disciples of *all nations*. . . (Matt. 28:18, 19).
>
> Go into *all the world* and preach the good news. . . And these *signs* will accompany. . . (Mark 16:15, 17).
>
> . . . and repentance and forgiveness of sins will be preached in his name to *all nations*. . . but stay in the city until you have been clothed with *power* from on high (Luke 24:47, 49).
>
> As the Father has sent me, I am *sending* you. . . . Receive the *Holy Spirit* (John 20:21, 22).
>
> But you will receive *power*. . . and you will be my *witnesses*. . . to the ends of the earth (Acts 1:8).

Charismatics sometimes chide evangelicals for "missing" these power promises linked to the Great Commission. Strangely, however, charismatics boldly claim these power promises without feeling the weight of the worldwide missionary mandate for which they are given.

Missions theology regarding the kingdom of God helps us to see the power promises in perspective. Missionary theologian Arthur F. Glasser of Fuller School of World Mission in Pasadena, California, teaches that these power manifestations are signs of the kingdom's triumph over the powers of darkness. As God's kingdom advances through the earth, it progressively destroys Satan's reign, blessing the redeemed with a foretaste of the blessings of God's eternal rule—liberation, healing and wholeness, peace and prosperity.

Missions theology also sees the potential of signs and wonders in terms of a dynamic known as "power encounter." Church Growth authority C. Peter Wagner defines power encounter as a "practical, visible demonstration that Jesus Christ is more powerful than the spirits, powers, or false gods worshiped or feared by the members of a given people group."[17] Such power demonstrations, both in history and today, are instrumental in turning whole segments of people groups to Christ. Great missionary advances will be made as more charismatics come to see the missionary implications of signs and wonders and spiritual gifts.

3. *Financial Prosperity.* Charismatic teaching on financial prosperity also needs to intersect with missions theology. A foundational tenet of the prosperity message is the idea of "the blessings of Abraham." Prosperity teachers recognize that Christians are Abraham's spiritual children and heirs to the blessings of the father of faith. But this Abrahamic inheritance is unpacked primarily in terms of material entitlements.

The theology of missions makes two points here. First, the promise to bless Abraham was only part of God's covenant with the patriarch. The other part of this covenant stipulated that Abraham was to *be a blessing*, and that through his descendants, all the peoples of the earth would be blessed. This extended blessing to all peoples is stressed no less than five times in the first book of the Bible (Gen. 12:3; 18:18; 22:18; 26:4–5; 28:14). Therefore, to claim the *blessings* of Abraham without taking seriously the mandate to *be a blessing* to all the peoples of the earth is to embrace only part of the covenant.

The second point is that while Abraham's blessings may include material wealth, it is significant that the central aspect of the blessings of Abraham in Paul's writings has to do with the salvation of the nations rather than material blessings for Christians.

> The scripture foresaw that God would *justify* the Gentiles by faith, and announced the *gospel* in advance to Abraham: "All nations will be blessed through you" (Gal. 3:8, emphasis mine).

Some charismatic leaders occasionally emphasize the missionary implications of the prosperity message. Faith teacher Kenneth Copeland, for example, defines prosperity as "the ability to use the power of God to meet the needs of mankind."[18] His wife, Gloria Copeland, has said that "we here in America are a blessed people financially. We have been called to finance the gospel to the world."[19] And *Charisma* editor Stephen Strang writes, "God does want to prosper his people. But He doesn't prosper us to feed our greed, but so we can be channels of His blessing to others and to spread the Gospel around the world."[20]

These challenges are encouraging, but they are both rare and poorly heeded. Statistics show that charismatic leaders in general have been poor stewards when it comes to "financing the gospel to the world." As mentioned earlier, even though charismatics are among the most generous givers to Christian causes, only a small percentage of their giving goes to world evangelization. Charismatic missions leader and author David Shibley says, "Of the top twenty U.S. churches in missions giving, not one of them is charismatic."[21] This is odd, especially in view of the fact that some of the largest and wealthiest churches in America and around the world are charismatic.

This stewardship failure suggests that the prosperity message is in captivity to the American dream. In affirming the biblical hope for blessing and prosperity, some have embraced what Stephen Strang calls "a convenient rationalization for those Christians who are simply greedy."[22] The prosperity message desperately needs to be brought into harmony with the worldwide missionary mandate connected to the blessings of Abraham.

4. Kingdom-Now. The "kingdom-now" message of Earl Paulk and others urges Christian penetration into secular society for the purpose of social transformation. A major block of mission theology deals with this issue under the rubric of the cultural mandate and its twin theme, the evangelistic mandate. The latter stresses the Great Commission and the spiritual needs of humanity. Both of these mandates are binding upon Christians. But if kingdom-now churches fail to distinguish between the two, they could easily supplant one for the sake of the other.

Addressing this issue, missions theology raises an important question. Which of these two mandates is priority? A major missiological document, the Lausanne Covenant, affirms both mandates but prioritizes evangelism:

> We affirm that Christ sends his redeemed people into the world as the Father sent him, and that this calls for a similar deep and costly penetration of the world. We need to break out of our ecclesiastical ghettos and permeate non-Christian society. In the church's mission of sacrificial service evangelism is primary.[23]

Kingdom-now theology could suffer imbalance if its teachers fail to distinguish between the kingdom of God and the church, and the relationship between the two. Here is where missions theology on the kingdom of God can help keep us from a humanistic triumphalism which confuses the kingdom and the church. The New Testament teaches that the kingdom is much bigger than the church. It came before the church. It created the church as its servant instrument.

"Kingdom-now" stresses the power of Christians to establish the kingdom in the world. "Taking dominion," or "taking the kingdom to the streets" are common charismatic slogans. According to the New Testament, however, it is not we who establish the kingdom. Rather, the kingdom establishes us and thrusts us into the world. The kingdom is not contingent upon us; we are contingent upon the kingdom. According to Jesus, the kingdom forcefully establishes itself on the earth by virtue of its own power—the mighty rule of God (Matt. 11:12). Our part is to seek this kingdom and press ourselves into it so that we in turn can become its instruments, signs, and servants, as it topples the kingdoms of this world (Luke 16:16). In other words, we do not take the kingdom to the streets, the kingdom takes *us* to the streets.

5. Restoration Theology. The restorationist teaching of People of Destiny International and other such groups can also be enhanced by what mission theology teaches about the missionary nature of the church, the nature of Paul's apostolic team, and the relationship between these two. We addressed this in chapter 7.

6. Discipleship/Shepherding Theology. The teachings of the shepherding stream of the independent charismatic movement similarly could benefit from missions theology on discipleship. Jesus' relationship to the twelve apostles as over against his relationship to a larger company of disciples—not to mention tax collectors and sinners—holds significance for Christian community. Also, how does the apostle Paul's model for training leaders differ from Jesus' approach? These and other missions theology issues would no doubt bring further balance and refinement to discipleship/shepherding theology.

The Importance of Theology. Why all this fuss about theology? Most charismatics prefer practical teaching and preaching over this kind of theological exercise. Most are impatient with theory. But theory is the driving force behind what we call "down to earth" and practical. There is a disproportionate amount of missionary activity in a movement as large as the charismatic one, and this shows the lack of a driving set of biblical, theological convictions about God's redemptive mission in the earth. This raises a hermeneutical concern.

A Hermeneutical Concern. How do we claim the blessing of Genesis 12:3 and fail to see that this "blessing of Abraham" does not stop with us, but is to be passed on by us to all the peoples of the earth? How do we teach about the power promised in the Gospels and Acts without stressing the Great Commission for which this power is given? And how do we claim the "fullness" of the Spirit without seeing global witness and harvest as the purpose of Pentecost? Such teaching is rampant in charismatic pulpits and television ministries across the nation. The problem is related to the fact that charismatics often expound their Bibles without the help of sound principles of biblical exegesis and hermeneutics.

Many influential charismatic pastors and teachers have been trained in seminary and consequently handle the Scriptures reasonably well. But by discouraging seminary training for others, they produce a second generation of independent charismatics who scoff at scholarship and insist that the Holy Spirit and "revelation knowledge" are all that one needs to interpret the Bible correctly. This failing threatens the movement even more than the highly publicized moral failures of the late 1980s.

Furthermore, how shall we "teach all nations" if we ourselves have not been properly schooled in biblical and theological disciplines? There is much to be learned from evangelicals, both in the area of mission theology and in the grammatical, historical approach to biblical interpretation.

What about evangelical missions theology itself? Can this discipline also be enriched by the theological and experiential distinctives of the charismatic movement?

CHARISMATIC TEACHING IMPACTS
THEOLOGY OF MISSION

In 1987 Howard Foltz presented a paper to the Society for Pentecostal Studies entitled "Moving Toward a Charismatic

Theology of Missions."[24] This paper shows several ways in which the distinctives of charismatic teaching and experience can and should impact current missions theology.

One way is to see the transdenominational unity of the charismatic movement as a key to cooperation in world evangelization. The charismatic emphasis on spiritual gifts is another way to enrich evangelical missions theology and practice. The gift-ministry of the Spirit is a key to missions motivation and mobilization and a corrective to our rationalistic, Western worldview, which is incompatible with most of the Third World. Foltz also shows how the teachings of the faith movement can impact missions theology and practice in positive ways:

> Faith teaching has elevated the expectations of many believers today to "attempt great things for God and expect great things from God." When dynamic rhema faith is released in reaching the nations, and not on selfish or material wants, great things can happen. Numerous missionaries from the faith movement have gone to the mission field and believed God for far more than the "average" missionary.[25]

Arnold Bittlinger, a Reformed pastor in Switzerland, has written an article entitled "The Significance of Charismatic Experiences for the Mission of the Church," in which he says:

> . . . Jesus talked and acted "charismatically." . . . Only if they, too, act charismatically can the disciples of Jesus continue his mission. For this purpose, the Holy Spirit is poured out upon them (Acts 1:8).[26]

There is no doubt that the charismatic movement and its distinctive teachings have much to contribute to missions theology and practice. At the same time, charismatics should allow current missions theology to influence their teachings and practices. The task of world evangelization requires the resources and energies of the whole church, not just one segment of it. The kind of exchange proposed in this chapter could help motivate both charismatic and noncharismatic churches toward becoming a blessing to all the nations of the world—a second blessing of a different sort.

NOTES

[1]Oswald J. Smith, *The Challenge of Missions* (Burlington, Ont.: Welch, 1984), p. 36.

[2]Howard Foltz, "Bottlenecks Hindering Missions Mobilization," *Ministries*, Vol. 4, No. 3, Summer 1986, p. 42.

[3]J. I. Packer, "Piety on Fire," *Christianity Today*, Vol. 33, No. 8, May 12, 1989, p. 20.

[4]Sources on some theological and cultural differences between Pentecostals and charismatics include Charles Farah, "Differences Within the Family," *Christianity Today*, Vol. 31, No. 15, Oct. 16, 1987, p. 25; Kenneth S. Kantzer, "Charismatics: Who Are We and What Do We Believe?" *Charisma*, Apr. 1980, p. 43; and Grant Wacker, "America's Pentecostals: Who They Are," *Christianity Today*, Vol. 31, No. 15, Oct. 16, 1987, p. 16.

[5]For a review of Renewal Theology see Mark Wilson, "Book Analysis: Theology from a Charismatic Perspective," and Jamie Buckingham, ed., "Meet the Author" in *Ministries Today*, Vol. 8, No. 1, Jan./Feb. 1990, pp. 78, 80.

[6]Dan R. McConnell, *A Different Gospel*(Peabody, Mass.: Hendrickson, 1988), p. xvii.

[7]Sources on "kingdom theology" and the movement include: Robert M. Bowman, et al., "The Gospel According to Paulk: A Critique of Kingdom Theology" (Part 1), *Christian Research Journal*, Vol. 8, No. 3, Winter/Spring 1988, p. 9; and Thomas F. Reid, "Understanding 'Kingdom Now' Teaching," *Ministries*, Vol. 4, No. 3, Summer 1986, p. 76.

[8]See Bowman, et al., "The Gospel," p. 13.

[9]David B. Barrett, "Statistics, Global," and Stephen Strang, "Simpson, Charles Vernon," in Stanley M. Burgess and Gary B. McGee, eds., *Dictionary of Pentecostal and Charismatic Movements* (Grand Rapids: Zondervan, 1988), p. 827 (Barrett), p. 787 (Strang).

[10]Bowman, et al., "The Gospel," p. 13; and Gary B. McGee, "Maranatha Campus Ministries, International," in Burgess and McGee, eds., *Dictionary*, p. 573.

[11]See P. D. Hocken, "The Charismatic Movement," in Burgess and McGee, eds., *Dictionary*, pp. 141–42, 157–58 (on restorationist currents in charismatic churches).

[12]See John Wimber with Kevin Springer, *Power Evangelism* (San Francisco, Calif.: Harper & Row, 1986).

[13]Howard Foltz, "Moving Toward a Charismatic Theology of Missions," *Probing Pentecostalism* (The Society for Pentecostal Studies, 17th Annual Meeting, Nov. 12–14, 1987, CBN University, Virginia Beach, Va.), pp. 76–77.

[14]See Roland Allen, *Missionary Principles* (Grand Rapids: Eerdmans, 1964), pp. 21, 30–38, 43, 137–38, 144–45.

[15]Ibid., pp. 144–45.

[16]A. B. Simpson, "When the Comforter Came" (Harrisburg, Pa.: Christian Publications, 1911), "The Thirtieth Day." Quoted and referenced as such in Gary B. McGee, *This Gospel Shall Be Preached*(Springfield, Mo.: Gospel Publishing House, 1989), pp. 58, 220.

[17]C. Peter Wagner, *How to Have a Healing Ministry Without Making Your Church Sick* (Ventura, Calif.: Regal Books, 1988), p. 150.

[18]Kenneth Copeland, *The Laws of Prosperity* (Fort Worth, Tex.: Kenneth Copeland Publications, 1974), p. 26; quoted by Allen Anderson in "The Prosperity Message in the Eschatology of Some New Charismatic Churches," *Missionalia*, Vol. 15, No. 2, 1987, p. 77.

[19]Gloria Copeland, *God's Will Is Prosperity* (Fort Worth, Tex.: Kenneth Copeland Publications, 1978), p. 45; quoted by Bruce Barron in *The Health and Wealth Gospel* (Downers Grove, Ill.: InterVarsity Press, 1987), p. 94.

[20]Stephen Strang, "A Few Thoughts on Prosperity and Greed: When is Enough Enough?" *Charisma & Christian Life*, Vol. 13, No. 3, Oct. 1987, p. 49.

[21]David Shibley, *A Force in the Earth* (Altamonte Springs, Fla.: Creation House, 1989), p. 94.

[22]Strang, "A Few Thoughts," p. 49.

[23]The Lausanne Covenant, International Congress on World Evangelization, Lausanne, Switzerland, July 1974, Article 6.

[24]Foltz, "Moving Toward," pp. 73–116.

[25]Ibid., pp. 101–2.

[26]Arnold Bittlinger, "The Significance of Charismatic Experiences for the Mission of the Church," *International Review Mission*, Vol. 75, No. 298, Apr. 1986, pp. 117–22.

Unleashing A More Effective Charismatic Missionary Force

Chapter 10

Roland Allen was one of the greatest missiologists of the twentieth century. He did not write from a Pentecostal perspective but as an Anglican whose mission theology was centered in the dynamic of the Holy Spirit. Church growth scholar John E. Branner observes,

> Allen's writings were produced long before the Charismatic Movement became worldwide, but they are suffused with its distinctive—that the world can be evangelized, not by the might of missions, or by the organizational and intellectual power of Christians, but by the Spirit of the living God.[1]

Allen saw no gulf between Spirit-led missions and the need for well-planned mission strategies. To him, the failure to find and use the best possible missionary methods was actually a denial of the Holy Spirit.[2] Allen was well aware of the Spirit's ability to transcend human methods. Contending for the spontaneity of the Spirit in missions, he decried the stuffy sacramentalism and institutionalization that characterized the contemporary ecclesiastical context. "Nevertheless," he argued, "the Spirit cannot be satisfied with any but the best methods."[3]

Allen's theological blending of the dynamic of the Spirit and human strategizing provides the perspective for what follows. It seems fitting to conclude this book on charismatic missions with a chapter on methods and strategies. In a sense, I am picking up where we left off earlier in describing a variety of charismatic missionary methods, but I will also pull together ideas from other discussions.

CAREY VERSUS CALVINISM: A CASE FOR STRATEGY

"Young man, sit down. When God pleases to convert the heathen, He will do it without your aid or mine."[4] This line echoes the hyper-Calvinism that pioneer mission strategist William Carey struggled against in the late eighteenth century.[5] Carey answered his opponents with a treatise entitled *An Enquiry into the Obligation of Christians to use Means for the Conversion of the Heathens* (1792). Using charts and a careful survey of the world, his Enquiry established the need for structures and strategies for missionary outreach.[6] To Carey, even a mariner's compass was a key tool for world evangelization.[7]

Charismatic Calvinism? A kind of neo-Calvinism prevails in some charismatic churches today, where the emphasis on the Holy Spirit preempts the need for research-based mission strategies. "Kind'a takes the Holy Spirit out of it," answered one charismatic evangelist, when I showed him some research on unreached people groups. But if we check our history, we will find where Pentecostal missions have excelled, there has been a healthy integration of the spontaneity of the Spirit and objective strategy planning.

Spirit and Strategy in Pentecostal Missions. Early in the Pentecostal movement, some zealous missionaries launched out strictly on the basis of their call and the urgency of the hour. They bypassed the need for training, fund raising, research on target groups, and strategic planning. Their impact, however, was short-lived and disappointing, according to Gary B. McGee, associate professor of Church History at the Assemblies of God Theological Seminary in Springfield, Missouri. "Many of these individuals failed overseas and returned home when their zeal faded."[8]

On the other hand, mission efforts by early Pentecostals who saw the need for training and strategic planning were more successful. Some of these were veterans of other missions agencies, and others received training in the early Pentecostal

Bible institutes that were springing up across the nation. McGee sums it up this way:

> As the Pentecostal Movement matured, more attention was placed on preparation for the foreign fields, sound financial support, and the necessity of an overall strategy to fulfill the Great Commission. This was particularly true with the developing Assemblies of God foreign missions program.[9]

Though some may never be convinced—not even by the arguments of a William Carey, a Roland Allen, or a Gary McGee—the phenomenal success of the Assemblies of God missions program to date should be enough in itself to convince charismatics of the need for an approach that combines both Spirit and strategy. Tensions between the emphases on the Holy Spirit and human strategy are inevitable. This final chapter assumes a blending of the two. The following recommendations are not a substitute for Spirit-led missions, but a supplement to Spirit-led missions. A prior context of prayer and sensitivity to the Spirit is assumed. In other words, what follows is a call for Spirit-led mission strategizing. If the emphasis falls on the human side of planning, it is because we assume the spiritual side is already being addressed.

STRUCTURES AND STRATEGIES FOR CHARISMATIC MISSIONS MOBILIZATION

The author is not proposing a prepackaged missions strategy. Instead, the following represents the kinds of issues that charismatic missions leaders will need to think through as they plan strategies. Specifically, charismatics organizing for missions will make decisions and establish some basic guidelines for effective missions planning in each of the following six areas.

1. Resolving the Issue of Structure. Entrepreneurs of charismatic missions will first need to decide what kinds of structures to use. Will the local church be the sending base? Or will separate or extra-local sending agencies be employed? Charismatics, we have seen, gravitate toward the "sending church" model. However, research confirms that there is virtually no such thing as a sending church capable of doing missions single-handedly.

Josh Peters, director of Globe Missionary Evangelism, has found that few charismatic churches are effective in sending out their own missionaries. He writes that

> If the home church has the personnel, time, money and commitment to the families they send out, some do very well. But most local churches, even the large ones, don't have the time or personnel to oversee the missionaries, meet their needs, so they can remain in good shape and stay on the field.[10]

Jim Zirkle of Living Water Teaching Missions makes a similar observation.

> Churches that want to have an internal [missions] program, if they are less than ten years old and less than 1,000 people, are headed for failure and trouble. . . . Virtually all churches, that I have seen, that have sent a missionary to the field, supporting him entirely, were the ruination of that missionary.[11]

As we saw in an earlier chapter, the more successful charismatic sending churches rely on various types of extra-local entities, such as training institutes, service agencies, indigenous ministries overseas, and the like. This seems to compromise the sending church ideal. But from a missiological perspective, reliance on extra-local missions structures *is* the biblical ideal.

For example, Paul's apostolic team was not the Antioch church doing missions from a distance. It was an autonomous, authoritative, extra-local mission structure, called forth and sent out by the Holy Spirit. New Testament churches impacted the world for Christ, not by becoming their own missions agencies, but by releasing and supporting God-ordained, extra-local missions structures to do what they themselves could not do.

Therefore, the ideal is not for every charismatic church to become a missions agency, but rather, to create extra-local sending structures or forge links with existing ones (such as those mentioned in chapter 7). Individual churches, however, are rarely equipped to create new missions agencies. A more efficient route, it seems, would be to consult or even join the Association of International Missions Services (AIMS) in Virginia Beach, Virginia. A charismatic organization, AIMS specializes in matching local churches with missions agencies of compatible vision and philosophy of ministry.

Networks of churches wanting to cooperate in missions can often supply the personnel and finances needed to set up their own training/sending agency. In such cases the Gulf States Missions Agency (highlighted in chapter 7) is a reproducible pattern that can work in similar networking situations. Network leaders, however, should consult AIMS for advice on starting a new sending agency. It may be that in the same region there already are existing charismatic agencies that can provide the necessary missions services, such as recruiting, training, placement, and supervision.

2. Recruiting and Training Missionary Candidates. Certain aspects of missionary recruitment and training are best handled by extra-local missions structures. Even so, the local church has a key role to play here. As we see in Acts, the apostle Paul recruited his team members from local churches.

A vibrant local church furnishes a most favorable environment for the formative years of a budding missionary candidate. Some vital functions of recruiting and training which can and should be performed under pastoral oversight in the local church are spiritual formation; apprenticeship training in ministry; discovery, development, and use of spiritual gifts; missions courses by correspondence; short-term missions trips; and final screening before turning candidates over to extra-local training/sending agencies.

The Gulf States Missions Agency in Reserve, Louisiana, uses a training pattern similar to these. Missionary candidates are selected in local churches with the pastor's cooperation and input. But before being accepted by Gulf States Missions, the candidate must be consistent in worship and spiritual growth, deeply involved in the life of the church, and involved in personal witnessing and evangelism. The candidate must work well as an apprentice in an older ministry, must submit to the pastor who also senses the candidate's missionary calling, must be a self-motivator who can pursue a clear vision, a team player who can maintain good relationships with co-workers, and must develop and use spiritual gifts responsibly.

The above criteria appear on a checklist to be approved by the missionary candidate's pastor. Only then is the candidate turned over to Gulf States Missions for the more advanced stages of training. (We described these stages in chapter 7.)

Some advanced training in Bible, missions, and the dynamics of cross-cultural ministry are essential. This is usually most effectively provided by structures that specialize in these areas. But local church input early in the process insures a harvest of church-centered missionaries who make potentially effective church planters.

For advanced missionary training, the Association of International Missions Services (AIMS) can recommend an appropriate training organization if starting a new one is not feasible. Also, charismatics should consider sending missionary candidates to accredited evangelical mission schools, such as Fuller Theological Seminary School of World Mission in Pasadena, California; Trinity Evangelical Divinity School in Deerfield, Illinois; and Biola University School of Intercultural Studies in La Mirada, California. Other accredited schools offering degree programs in missions include Asbury Theological Seminary, Columbia Graduate School of Bible and Missions, Wheaton Graduate School, Dallas Theological Seminary, and Moody Bible Institute.

3. Developing Field Selection Theory. Placing missionaries on the field requires the expertise of translocal missions structures. The home church may designate a particular continent or country, but within a given nation there may be dozens or hundreds of hidden people groups overlooked by national churches or missionaries serving there. It is not unusual to find charismatic missionaries involved in clusters of church development while nearby ripened harvest fields lack laborers.

What is needed in many charismatic churches and missions agencies is a sound theory of field selection based on the unreached-peoples approach, as over against a geographical approach. For example, one missionary may say, "I am called to China." But another may say, "I am called to reach Mandarin-speaking Chinese living in the Greater Los Angeles area of California." The latter is more focused.

The people approach to world evangelization has biblical foundations. The apostle Paul was not called to a region as such. He labored particularly among Greek-speaking Gentiles of the Roman world who had some connections to Jewish synagogues. But the apostles at Jerusalem, namely James, Peter, and John, initially concentrated mainly on fellow Jews.

The people approach, addressed later in this chapter as a major trend, has clarified the modern missionary task perhaps more than any other missiological tool. For the most part, even those who question it on biblical, exegetical grounds agree that the people approach is the best way to plan for world evangelization.[12] Research agencies, such as the Global Mapping Project in Pasadena, California, and Missions Advanced Research and Communication Center (MARC) in Monrovia, California, can supply information on people groups around the world. Armed with this kind of insight and information, sending agencies can tell where missionaries are most needed in a given country.

Also, owing to an inadequate grasp of field selection theory, there is a lack of clarity in some charismatic churches as to the meaning of home missions. For example, if an Anglo-American church in New Orleans, Louisiana, evangelizes Arabic speaking Muslims living in the same city, this is truly a missionary task, which some would call home missions.

However, for a church to use missions funds to install new carpet or pave its parking lot is not home missions and should not be called that.

Various types of social ministries are also called home missions by some charismatics. These are part of the biblical cultural mandate. However, the biblical command to make disciples of all nations takes priority over the cultural mandate. And while both mandates are part of missions and binding on all Christians, failure to delineate between the two often results in the neglect of the evangelistic mandate. While all strategy suggestions given here are for the evangelistic mandate, this does not signify a lack of concern for the cultural mandate. The latter is important, but it is simply not the subject at hand.

4. Setting Goals and Planning Strategies. Charismatic missionaries often attach themselves to existing churches overseas, filling positions that could just as easily be filled by nationals for a fraction of the cost. Where this is true, the charismatic missionary force has lost its apostolic edge and turned instead to church development. This problem stems from the lack of a well-planned missions strategy. A clearly defined missions strategy might include the following steps:

Identify an unreached people that is receptive to the Gospel.

Recruit and train a missionary force to reach them.

Deploy the missionary force, having set clear goals for evangelism, church planting, and leadership training.

Monitor the progress and evaluate the results in terms of countable new churches, disciples, and leaders.

When the people group is "reached," redeploy the missionary force to another receptive, unreached people group.[13]

C. Peter Wagner has written, "Time and again research has confirmed that planting new churches is the most effective evangelistic methodology known under heaven."[14] The greatest need in missions today is for a few good missionaries to penetrate unreached people groups and plant indigenous churches that can grow and multiply within those groups and evangelize cross-culturally beyond their own people. Seen this way, the missionary task is not so formidable. Missions strategist Ralph D. Winter of the U.S. Center for World Mission in Pasadena, California, says,

> Our goal is not to raise up enough missionaries to knock on the doors of each one of the almost three billion unsaved, but to establish national churches—"missionary beachheads"—where the local, ethnic church can do the mop-up "knocking on doors."[15]

An effective overseas missions strategy might also focus on leadership training—a major component of Paul's missionary strategy in the first century and a mammoth challenge in modern missions. Some charismatic leaders see this as one of the greatest needs in missions today. David Shibley, former missions director at Church on the Rock in Rockwall, Texas, says, "Where strong national churches exist, our method is to augment and strengthen these, helping them to see their evangelistic and missionary responsibilities."[16] Dolly Davis, missions secretary at Billy Joe Daugherty's Victory Christian Center in Tulsa, Oklahoma, says, "We believe strongly, and everybody I talk to is leaning this way: train the nationals; train the pastors."[17]

To maximize effectiveness, however, a leadership training strategy should include an apprenticeship element, keeping frontier evangelism and church planting clearly in focus. We are not interested in training armchair theologians, but rather men and women who want to evangelize their own people and reach out cross-culturally to neighboring unreached people groups.

In some situations it may be better to train people within their own country rather than extracting them from their ministry environment. According to Johan Engelbrecht, president of the Institute for Church Growth in Africa, eighty-five percent of Africans who come to the United States for ministry training stay here instead of returning to minister among their own people.[18] This is a shameful proportion. One charismatic organization, Christ for the Nations Institute (CFNI) in Dallas, Texas, responds to the brain drain in this way:

> Concerned that many foreign students, as well as students from areas lacking strong charismatic presence, were being taken from their environment never to return, CFNI has been instrumental in establishing Bible schools in Bad Gandersheim (West Germany), Montego Bay (Jamaica), and New York City (Long Island). CFNI alumni have established schools modeled after CFNI in Argentina, Finland, Mexico, Malaysia, Spain, and Thailand.[19]

5. Directing and Supervising Missionaries. The ideal of the sending church pastoring and directing its own missionaries without extra-local assistance is just that—an ideal. It rarely works. For example, we have already looked at Victory World Missions Outreach (VWMO), led by Gary Rechtfertig in Tulsa, Oklahoma. This is a charismatic service agency which leaves authority over missionaries in the hands of the sending and receiving churches. But in 1989 Gary visited all of VWMO's missionaries in Europe and Africa and found many of them in need of pastoral care. The home churches were not carrying that responsibility. "Out of the thirty or forty churches behind our people," says Gary, "I can only think of one pastor who's been to the field specifically to visit their missionary."[20]

To hold missionaries properly accountable, some churches have found it beneficial to entrust them to the care of extra-local missions structures or indigenous ministries on the field. For example, charismatic churches that send missionaries out under Globe Missionary Evangelism release their missionaries to the authority of the mission. Globe, in turn, appoints field directors in foreign countries as needed.

Similarly, authority over missionaries of Living Water Teaching is clearly in the hands of the mission. Jim Zirkle, director of Living Water Teaching, sees himself as a pastor to his missionaries. He says, "All of those with our organization [in the city where I live] go to church because I am their pastor. If I cannot be their pastor, then I cannot be their director."[21]

Like Zirkle, most charismatics feel strongly that missionaries, like ministers, need spiritual covering and oversight. But in the emerging charismatic missionary movement, the lines of accountability are sometimes fuzzy. Charismatic missions leaders, because of their emphasis on the Spirit's leading, are careful not to strong-arm their missionaries. But some have learned the hard way that there is no substitute for good, old-fashioned accountability. Before a young missionary even gets a passport, everyone involved should be perfectly clear as to "where the buck stops."

6. Evaluating Missions and Missionaries. Years ago a missions director of a well-known evangelical mission decided to evaluate 150 missionaries under his care. When the missionaries heard about it, half of them resigned.[22] Evaluation is not a popular exercise but a necessary one.

Three basic aspects of evaluation are goals, methods, and results. If the goal of the mission or missionaries is evangelism and church planting, then the criteria of evaluation must include a measurable harvest of new churches and disciples. If there is no harvest, the methods employed and perhaps the missionaries themselves need examining.

Charismatics often play down the relationship between methods and results. Some accept the idea that if we are praying, fasting, and "pulling down strongholds," God will grace any method with spectacular results. This is not so. It has been documented that, while right methods reap bountiful harvests even where the reapers are *not* charismatic, manifestations of spiritual power *do not* automatically produce a harvest.[23] Roland Allen, a pioneer in Spirit-centered mission theology, has this word of wisdom:

> Apparent failure should certainly lead us to question whether we were manifesting the Spirit of Christ in a right way. It is a dangerous delusion which persists in using

methods which apparently fail, on the plea that we ought not to think of results. Such a doctrine would justify the most stupid methods. If we go forth in the Spirit we ought to expect to see results. If we do not see good results, our first duty is to question our methods. . . . To go on labouring without any apparent success may be the height of faith or the depth of stubborn self-will.[24]

In his book *Strategies for Church Growth*, C. Peter Wagner tells the story of a pastor and his team who knocked on four thousand doors in one year as part of their evangelistic strategy. The results were nil. No converts. So the next year they set out to knock on eight thousand doors. "The program was supreme," quips Wagner, "even though it was producing no results."[25]

Charismatics need to think seriously about evaluation of missionaries and their methods in terms of results. Time and again charismatic missions leaders have been asked, "What do your missionaries do on the field?" Sometimes it is difficult to get straight answers, especially in terms of clearly stated goals, clearly defined methods, and clearly documented results. When asked about the activities of one missionary, a certain missions director replied, "He's missionizing." One can only guess the meaning of "missionizing."

Evaluation is one of the indispensable keys to an effective missionary force. It takes time and research and requires integrity. Evaluation requires a firm willingness to face up to and weed out allegedly "value free" methods. In a world of spiritual darkness where even the best methods are not sufficient in themselves, we dare not settle for anything less than the best possible methods. On this point, Roland Allen has written that

> Refusal to study the best methods, refusal to regard organization as of any importance, is really not the denial of matter, but the denial of the Spirit. It is sloth, not faith.[26]

We have considered structure, recruiting and training, field selection, goal setting and strategy planning, supervision, and evaluation. These are just a few of the issues that charismatics organizing for missions will face. There are more. Left unmentioned are missions education and awareness for the local church. Also, major decisions will need to be made about financing for missions and missionaries. For further insight and information on the dynamics of missions strategy and mobilization, especially from a charismatic perspective, I once again point in the direction of Howard Foltz and the Association of International Missions Services (AIMS) in Virginia Beach, Virginia.

WORLD TRENDS TO BE RECKONED WITH

We have repeatedly stressed that a major dynamic of spiritual renewal is the creation of new patterns of ministry and missions for a new world. We have looked at several major developments related to the charismatic renewal, including the emergence of independent charismatic churches, networking among these churches, the trend toward church-based missions, and the creation of extra-local missions structures by charismatics. To keep in step with the spirit of renewal, we need to constantly evaluate and adjust present missions strategies in light of current and foreseeable global changes. If we ignore these changes, clinging to current methods, our effectiveness will soon fade.

Effective missions leadership for today and tomorrow requires a perspective that is both worldwide and world-wise. It seems fitting to close this book on charismatic missions by pointing to some of the mammoth changes around the globe that will drastically impact missions strategies for the 1990s and beyond. The implications of the trends mentioned below are far too broad to spell out in detail, but I hope these will inspire further study on the part of the readers involved in planning missions strategy.

1. *People Group Thinking.* The people approach to world evangelization is strategically important. A brief overview of people group thinking and its implications for missions strategy would include the following.

A *people group* is a fairly large group of individuals who relate together and share common social and cultural characteristics. An *unreached* people group is one which has no Christian community of sufficient numbers and resources to reach the entire group without outside, cross-cultural assistance. They are not likely to receive the Gospel from Christians in neighboring people groups unless those Christians are able to bridge the cultural differences. Missionaries are needed to do this.

Today's three billion unevangelized people include a vast mosaic of some twelve thousand *unreached people groups.* A given country may have dozens or even thousands of such groups. Therefore, even though churches may exist in every nation, the world is not fully evangelized.

At any given time, some people groups are more open to the Gospel than others. An effective global evangelization strategy will include the sending of cross-cultural missionaries to plant indigenous, multiplying churches within responsive unreached people groups wherever they are found. Current data on unreached peoples and their openness to the Gospel may be obtained from research agencies such as the Global Mapping Project in Pasadena, California.

These and other concepts in people group thinking have been developed by leading missiologists including Edward R. Dayton and John D. Robb of World Vision International, Donald A. McGavran and C. Peter Wagner of Fuller Theological Seminary, School of World Mission, and Ralph D. Winter of the U.S. Center for World Mission.[27] As more charismatics catch on to this revolutionary focus in missions, their effectiveness will increase. The charismatic-oriented Association of International Missions Services (AIMS) in Virginia Beach, Virginia, stresses the people approach to world missions.

2. *The Globalization of World Missions.* The term "emerging Third World missions" is a misnomer. According to Larry Pate,

a leading authority on non-Western missions, Third World missions have already emerged.[28] Indigenous churches around the world are spawning their own missionary movements. Asia, for example, now sponsors 17,300 missionaries involved in cross-cultural outreach among unreached people groups.[29] The cost and cultural complexities for Third World missions are much less than they are for Western missions.

Unleashing a more effective missionary force demands that both charismatics and noncharismatics rethink the role of the Western missionary in light of Third World missions. New patterns for networking and partnering between Western and Third World missions are now emerging. Increasingly, Western missionaries will find themselves specializing in specific missionary activities. According to Pate, key areas of specialization already include training of Third World missionaries, pioneer church planting, research/strategy specialization, and church growth specialization.[30]

3. *The World a Global City.* Soon the majority of the world's population will be urban dwellers. Already major metropolitan centers such as Los Angeles, Sydney, Tokyo, and other cities of the Pacific Rim are impacting and shaping the world's economic, social, and cultural landscape. As the masses stream into the cities, their openness to a new way of life and to a new faith peaks. This presents one of the greatest challenges and opportunities the church has ever witnessed. Serious thinkers about missions strategy are coming to terms with the implications of urbanization. As urban missiologist Roger S. Greenway concludes, ". . .at no time in history has it been more true than now that he who wins the city, wins the world."[31]

4. *The Rise of the Pacific Rim.* As the third millennium dawns, the world's demographic, political, cultural, and economic power base will no longer be the Atlantic, but the Pacific Rim—those lands whose coastlines meet the waters of the Pacific Ocean. "The Pacific Rim is emerging like a dynamic

young America but on a much grander scale," write leading trend-watchers John Naisbitt and Patricia Aburdene.[32]

This massive, global shift is paralleled by changes in the spiritual realm and in the church. Already, we have noted, Third World missions will soon outgrow the Western missionary force as far as numbers are concerned. But these changes need not signal a sideline role for the Western missionary force, unless we ignore the implications of the shift and fail to adapt our strategies accordingly.

5. The Fall of the Iron Curtain. McDonald's hamburgers are now sold in Moscow's Red Square. Sadly, hours after the Berlin Wall opened up pornography was on the magazine racks in East Germany. The trend toward democratization and free-market socialism in Eastern Europe, the Soviet Union, Mongolia, and China opens up new vistas for the church as well. As the masses taste new freedom, they will be particularly open to the Gospel. "Chinese and Soviet young people are fascinated by religion," write Naisbitt and Aburdene, "and enjoy attending church to the dismay of their Communist-schooled elders."[33] The strategic opportunity and challenge sounded by these changes are enormous. But time is not on our side. The doors can close as fast as we have seen them open, as the August 1991 coup attempt in the Soviet Union illustrates.

6. Missions to America. Secularization, urbanization, the rise of youth culture, the New Age movement, and the massive immigration of foreign peoples into the United States make our country a mission field once again. Strategies for penetrating urban or youth culture, for instance, are no less missionary in nature than strategies for evangelizing unreached people groups overseas. Likewise, for Americans to reach new ethnic populations coming here will require cross-cultural missions training and strategy. In addition to local evangelistic outreach, where a church wins and disciples its own kind of people, real missionary strategies are needed for evangelism and church planting among diverse segments of society within the church's sphere of outreach.

These are some of the sweeping changes to be reckoned with by any movement wanting to stay on the cutting edge of world evangelization. Naisbitt and Aburdene write, "In turbulent times, in times of great change, people head for two extremes: fundamentalism and personal, spiritual experience."[34] To what spiritual experience will today's searching masses turn? Much depends on the church's ability to seize its global opportunities and point the way to Jesus Christ and the kingdom of God.

Other current trends in the church include an increasing emphasis on prayer and spiritual warfare, and the merging of a charismatic and noncharismatic missionary force. More and more charismatics are seeing the need to adopt missiological tools and strategies largely pioneered by noncharismatic evangelicals. Conversely, evangelicals are increasingly recognizing the spiritual realm as the real battlefield in world evangelization. As both sides come together, matching strategic excellence with spiritual power, the world will witness a new—perhaps the final—age of missions.

NOTES

[1]John E. Branner, "Roland Allen: Pioneer in a Spirit-Centered Theology of Mission," *Missiology, An International Review*, Vol. V, No. 2, Apr. 1977, p. 175.

[2]Roland Allen, *Missionary Principles* (Grand Rapids: Eerdmans, 1964), p. 133.

[3]Ibid., p. 130.

[4]Ruth A. Tucker, *From Jerusalem to Irian Jaya* (Grand Rapids: Zondervan, 1983), p. 115.

[5]Stephen Neill, *A History of Christian Missions* (New York: Penguin Books, 1964), p. 261.

[6]An excerpt of Carey's *Enquiry* is found in Ralph D. Winter and Steven C. Hawthorne, eds., *Perspectives on the World Christian Movement* (Pasadena, Calif.: William Carey Library, 1981), p. 227.

[7]Edward R. Dayton and David A. Fraser, *Planning Strategies for World Evangelization* (Grand Rapids: Eerdmans, 1980), p. 280.

[8]Gary B. McGee, *This Gospel Shall Be Preached* (Springfield, Mo.: GospelPublishing House, 1989), p. 86.

[9]Gary B. McGee, "Early Pentecostal Missionaries—They Went

Everywhere Preaching the Gospel," in Grant L. McClung, ed., *Azusa Street and Beyond* (South Plainfield, N.J.: Bridge, 1986), p. 36.

[10]Telephone interview, August 9, 1988.

[11]Interview, June 21, 1989.

[12]See David J. Hesselgrave, *Today's Choices for Tomorrow's Mission* (Grand Rapids, Mich.: Zondervan Publishing House, 1988), pp. 51–52.

[13]Adapted from a model proposed in Dayton and Fraser, *Planning Strategies*, pp. 43–47.

[14]C. Peter Wagner, *Spiritual Power and Church Growth* (Altamonte Springs, Fla.: Strang Communications, 1986), p. 56.

[15]Ralph D. Winter quoted by Larry Tomczak in "The World Mission of Every Christian," *People of Destiny*, Vol. 4, No. 5, Sept./Oct. 1986, p. 17. See also C. Peter Wagner, *Strategies for Church Growth* (Ventura, Calif.: Regal Books, 1987). On p. 185 Wagner says, "The statement 'nationals can evangelize better than missionaries' is correct. The job of the cross-cultural missionary is to establish a beachhead to lead some to Christ, to nurture them in Christian formation and to motivate them to move out to evangelize their own people and multiply Christian churches."

[16]Interview, June 25, 1989.

[17]Interview, June 22, 1989.

[18]Interview, June 19, 1989.

[19]David D. Bundy, "Christ For The Nations Institute," in Stanley M. Burgess and Gary B. McGee, eds., *Dictionary of Pentecostal and Charismatic Movements* (Grand Rapids: Zondervan, 1988), p. 162.

[20]Telephone interview, February 16, 1990.

[21]Jim Zirkle, *Missions: The How To, Part IV—Standards* (Tulsa, Okla.: Jim Zirkle, n.d.), p. 22.

[22]Larry Tomczak, "The World Mission," p. 17.

[23]See C. Peter Wagner, "Church Growth," in Burgess and McGee, eds., *Dictionary*, pp. 184–85.

[24]Allen, *Missionary Principles*, pp. 57–58.

[25]Wagner, *Planning Strategies*, p. 33.

[26]Allen, *Missionary Principles*, p. 133.

[27]See Dayton and Fraser, *Planning Strategies*, pp. 107ff.; Ralph D. Winter, "Unreached Peoples: The Development of a Concept" in Harvie M. Conn, ed., *Reaching the Unreached* (Phillipsburg, N.J.: Presbyterian and Reformed Publishing Co., 1984), p. 37; John D. Robb, *Focus: The Power of People Group Thinking* (Monrovia, Calif.: MARC, 1989); C. Peter Wagner, *Strategies for Church Growth*, pp. 57–93; and Donald A. McGavran, *Understanding Church Growth* (Grand Rapids: Eerdmans, 1980).

[28]Larry Pate, *From Every People* (Monrovia, Calif.: MARC, 1989), p. 13.

[29]Ibid., p. 26.

[30]Larry Pate, *The Globalization of World Evangelism*, (unpublished manuscript, 1990), pp. 82–85.

[31]Roger S. Greenway, *Apostles to the City*, (Grand Rapids: Baker, 1978), p. 11.

[32]John Naisbitt and Patricia Aburdene, *Megatrends 2000: Ten New Directions for the 1990s* (New York: William Morrow, 1990), p. 178.

[33]Ibid., p. 271.

[34]Ibid., p. 277.

INDEX

VWMTC (Victory World Missions Training Center), 99, 114, 123
Wacker, Grant, 47, 137
Wagner, C. Peter, 20, 40, 71, 72, 83, 117, 120, 126, 158, 175, 179, 181
Waldensians, 112
Watt, Eric, 89
Weiner, Bob, 27, 41, 67, 153
Wheaton Graduate School, 173
White, Gordon, 102
Wilkerson, David, 27, 34
Wilkerson, Ralph, 38
Willhite, B.J., 68
Williams, J. Rodman, 151
Wimber, John, 41, 67, 154
Winter, Ralph D., 82, 83, 142, 176
Witnessing, 128
Women's movement, 63

Word churches, 67, 68
Word of Faith Church, 65
Working theology, 52–53
World Fellowship of Ministers, 65
World Indigenous Missions, 88, 122–23
World Outreach Ministries, 124–25
World Vision International, 181
Wycliffe Bible Translators, 88, 100

Youth With a Mission (YWAM), 55, 89, 98, 100, 117, 121–22, 144, 145

Zachary, Rick, 95
Zirkle, Jerry, 115
Zirkle, Jim, 104, 105, 115, 171, 177–78
Zondervan Publishing House, 151